# LOU GEHRIG

**Titles in the Series**
**Baseball's All-Time Greatest Hitters**

Hank Aaron

Barry Bonds

Ty Cobb

Joe DiMaggio

Lou Gehrig

Rogers Hornsby

Joe Jackson

Willie Mays

Stan Musial

Pete Rose

Babe Ruth

Ted Williams

WILLIAM C. KASHATUS

BASEBALL'S ALL-TIME GREATEST HITTERS

GREENWOOD PRESS
WESTPORT, CONNECTICUT • LONDON

**Library of Congress Cataloging-in-Publication Data**

Kashatus, William C., 1959–
Lou Gehrig : a biography / William C. Kashatus.
p. cm.—(Baseball's all-time greatest hitters)
Includes bibliographical references and index.
ISBN 0–313–32866–8 (alk. paper)
1. Gehrig, Lou, 1903–1941. 2. Baseball players—United States—Biography. I. Title. II. Series.
GV865.G4K37 2004
796.357'092—dc22 2004040448
[B]

British Library Cataloguing in Publication Data is available.



Library of Congress Catalog Card Number: 2004040448
ISBN: 0–313–32866–8

First published in 2004

Greenwood Press, 88 Post Road West, Westport, CT 06881
An imprint of Greenwood Publishing Group, Inc.
www.greenwood.com

Printed in the United States of America

The paper used in this book complies with the Permanent Paper Standard issued by the National Information Standards Organization (Z39.48–1984).

10 9 8 7 6 5 4 3 2 1

To the memories of
William C. Kashatus, Sr., and John Markiewicz, Sr.

# Contents

# Series Foreword

The volumes in Greenwood's "Baseball's All-Time Greatest Hitters" series present the life stories of the players who, through their abilities to hit for average, for power, or for both, most helped their teams at the plate. Much thought was given to the players selected for inclusion in this series. In some cases, the selection of certain players was a given. **Ty Cobb**, **Rogers Hornsby**, and **Joe Jackson** hold the three highest career averages in baseball history: .367, .358, and .356, respectively. **Babe Ruth**, who single-handedly brought the sport out of its "dead ball" era and transformed baseball into a home-run hitters game, hit 714 home runs (a record that stood until 1974) while also hitting .342 over his career. **Lou Gehrig**, now known primarily as the man whose consecutive-games record Cal Ripken Jr. broke in 1995, hit .340 and knocked in more than 100 runs eleven seasons in a row, totaling 1,995 before his career was cut short by ALS. **Ted Williams**, the last man in either league to hit .400 or better in a season (.406 in 1941), is widely regarded as possibly the best hitter ever, a man whose fanatical dedication raised hitting to the level of both science and art.

Two players set career records that, for many, define the art of hitting. **Hank Aaron** set career records for home runs (755) and RBIs (2,297). He also maintained a .305 career average over twenty-three seasons, a remarkable feat for someone primarily known as a home-run hitter. **Pete Rose** had ten seasons with 200 or more hits and won three batting titles on his way to establishing his famous record of 4,256 career hits. Some critics have claimed that both players' records rest more on longevity than excellence. To that I would say there is something to be said about longevity and, in both cases, the player's excellence was the reason why he had the opportunity to keep playing, to keep tallying hits for his team. A base hit is the mark of a successful plate appearance; a home run is the apex of an at-bat. Accordingly, we could hardly have a series titled "Baseball's All-Time Greatest Hitters" without including the two men who set the career records in these categories.

**Joe DiMaggio** holds another famous mark: fifty-six consecutive games in which he obtained a base hit. Many have called this baseball's most unbreakable record. (The player who most closely approached that mark was Pete Rose, who hit safely in forty-four consecutive games in 1978.) In his thirteen seasons, DiMaggio hit .325 with 361 home runs and 1,537 RBIs. This means he *averaged* 28 home runs and 118 RBIs per season. MVPs have been awarded to sluggers in various years with lesser stats than what DiMaggio achieved in an "average" season.

Because **Stan Musial** played his entire career with the Cardinals in St. Louis—once considered the western frontier of the baseball world in the days before baseball came to California—he did not receive the press of a DiMaggio. But Musial compiled a career average of .331, with 3,630 hits (ranking fourth all time) and 1,951 RBIs (fifth all time). His hitting prowess was so respected around the league that Brooklyn Dodgers fans once dubbed him "The Man," a nickname he still carries today.

**Willie Mays** was a player who made his fame in New York City and then helped usher baseball into the modern era when he moved with the Giants to San Francisco. Mays did everything well and with flair. His over-the-shoulder catch in the 1954 World Series was perhaps his most famous moment, but his hitting was how Mays most tormented his opponents. Over twenty-two seasons the "Say Hey Kid" hit .302 and belted 660 home runs.

Only four players have reached the 600-home-run milestone: Mays, Aaron, Ruth, and **Barry Bonds**, who achieved that feat in 2002. Bonds, the only active player included in this series, broke the single-season home-run record when he smashed 73 for the San Francisco Giants in 2001. In the 2002 National League Championship Series, St. Louis Cardinals pitchers were so leery of pitching to him that they walked him ten times in twenty-one plate appearances. In the World Series, the Anaheim Angels walked him thirteen times in thirty appearances. He finished the Series with a .471 batting average, an on-base percentage of .700, and a slugging percentage of 1.294.

As with most rankings, this series omits some great names. Jimmie Foxx, Tris Speaker, and Tony Gwynn would have battled for a hypothetical thirteenth volume. And it should be noted that this series focuses on players and their performance within Major League Baseball; otherwise, sluggers such as Josh

Gibson from the Negro Leagues and Japan's Sadaharu Oh would have merited consideration.

There are names such as Cap Anson, Ed Delahanty, and Billy Hamilton who appear high up on the list of career batting average. However, a number of these players played during the late 1800s, when the rules of baseball were drastically different. For example, pitchers were not allowed to throw overhand until 1883, and foul balls weren't counted as strikes until 1901 (1903 in the American League). Such players as Anson and company undeniably were the stars of their day, but baseball has evolved greatly since then, into a game in which hitters must now cope with night games, relief pitchers, and split-fingered fastballs.

Ultimately, a list of the "greatest" anything is somewhat subjective, but Greenwood offers these players as twelve of the finest examples of hitters throughout history. Each volume focuses primarily on the playing career of the subject: his early years in school, his years in semi-pro and/or minor league baseball, his entrance into the majors, and his ascension to the status of a legendary hitter. But even with the greatest of players, baseball is only part of the story, so the player's life before and after baseball is given significant consideration. And because no one can exist in a vacuum, the authors often take care to recreate the cultural and historical contexts of the time—an approach that is especially relevant to the multidisciplinary ways in which sports are studied today.

Batter up.

**ROB KIRKPATRICK**
**GREENWOOD PUBLISHING**
**FALL 2003**

# Chronology

**1903** Born Henry Louis Gehrig in New York City on June 19.

**1920** Hits home run for Commerce High School in national high school championship played at Wrigley field against Lane Tech of Chicago; Gehrig is dubbed the "Babe Ruth of the school yards."

**1923** Plays his only baseball season with Columbia University, hitting .444 with 7 home runs in the nineteen-game college season; signs with the New York Yankees for $3,500; strikes out in first major league at-bat on June 18; collects first major league base hit on July 19; hits first major league home run on September 27.

**1925** Starts consecutive game streak with a pinch-hitting appearance on June 1.

**1926** Plays in his first World Series, collecting 10 hits and 3 RBIs for a .348 average.

**1927** Wins first American League RBI title with 175; named league's Most Valuable Player.

**1928** Plays in his third straight World Series and hits .545 with 4 home runs and 9 RBIs, one of the best Series performances of all time.

**1931** Wins first American League home-run title with 46; sets the all-time league record of 184 RBIs in a single season; named league MVP by the *Sporting News*.

**1932** Becomes first American Leaguer to hit 4 home runs in a game, on June 3.

**1933** Plays first base for the American League in the first All-Star Game; marries Eleanor Twitchell on September 29.

**1934** Plays in 1,308th consecutive game on August 17, breaking the previous record held by Everett Scott; wins the American League's Triple Crown; named league MVP by the *Sporting News*.

**1936** Named American League's MVP for capturing his third home-run title; named the league's MVP by the Baseball Writers of America.

**1939** Ends his consecutive game streak at 2,130 when he removes himself from the starting line-up on May 2; visits the Mayo Clinic where he learns that he has amyotrophic lateral sclerosis (ALS) on June 19; honored at Yankee Stadium where he delivers his famed farewell speech on July 4; inducted into the National Baseball Hall of Fame after the usual waiting period is waived; becomes first Yankee player to have his uniform number retired.

**1941** Dies of ALS at home in the Riverdale section of New York City on June 2.

# Introduction

On July 4, 1939, more than 60,000 fans packed New York's Yankee Stadium to honor one of the greatest baseball players of all time, Lou Gehrig. A corps of newspaper reporters and photographers crowded in to capture the historic moment, and the first baseman's past and current teammates gathered to pay him tribute. The guest list read like the starting line-up of an All Star Game—Babe Ruth, Bill Dickey, Tony Lazzeri, and Joe DiMaggio—men who had captured the hearts and imaginations of every youth who ever dreamed of becoming a major leaguer.[1]

Showered with gifts and praise from manager to bat boy, Gehrig reached for a handkerchief and, fighting back tears, made his way to the microphone. Cap in hand, he scanned the crowd of well-wishers and then began to speak: "Fans, for the past two weeks you've been reading about the bad break I got. Yet today I consider myself the luckiest man on the face of the earth."[2] A hushed silence engulfed the stadium. Cameras flashed. Memories flooded minds, and grown men wept unabashedly for a childhood hero.

"I've been in ballparks for seventeen years and I never received anything but kindness and encouragement from you fans." The Yankee slugger spoke surprisingly clearly, without notes—straight from the heart. After recalling the close friendships he had made during his professional career, Gehrig attempted to place his remarkable life in perspective: "When you have a father and mother who work all their lives so that you can have an education and build your body, it's a blessing. When you have a wife who has been a tower of strength and shown more courage than you dreamed existed, that's the finest I know."

Lou Gehrig being honored by the Yankees, Washington Senators, and more than 61,000 fans who gathered at Yankee Stadium on July 4, 1939. *The Sporting News.*

"So I close in saying that I may have had a tough break," he concluded, "but I have an awful lot to live for."[3]

Later that year, the Yankees retired Gehrig's uniform number 4—making him the first player in history to receive that honor—and the Baseball Writers Association waived an eligibility rule so that they could elect Gehrig to the National Baseball Hall of Fame.[4] Two years later, at the age of 37, Lou Gehrig died of amyotrophic lateral sclerosis (ALS), the disease that today bears his name.

Few realized that during his long and stellar career the adored Yankee hero openly wept when he lost games and he lived in constant fear that his talent would desert him.[5] At 6 feet and 200 pounds, Gehrig, who signed with the Yankees in 1923, possessed a rock-solid physique that enabled him to become the premier clean-up hitter in the American League for most of his seventeen-year career. Year in and year out, he hit the ball with power, batting more than

.300 and almost always driving in more than 100 runs. Gehrig won five American League RBI titles, including a 184-RBI explosion in 1931 that still stands as an American League record. Just as impressive are his .340 lifetime average and 493 career home runs. With Gehrig as their clean-up hitter and first baseman, the Yankees captured seven pennants and six world championships. His .361 batting average, 10 home runs, and 35 RBIs in World Series competition still rank among the very best performances in the history of the Fall Classic.[6]

But for all his achievements, Lou Gehrig was overshadowed by his more popular teammates, Babe Ruth and Joe DiMaggio. Happy to surrender the spotlight, Gehrig, who was withdrawn, modest, and unassuming by nature, accepted his subordinate position without envy or resentment, admitting that he wasn't "a headline guy, just the guy on the Yankees who's in there every day."[7]

But Gehrig had something that Ruth or DiMaggio couldn't touch: the major league record for most consecutive games played. From June 2, 1925, to May 2, 1939, he appeared in every game the New York Yankees played. Shaking off injuries, illnesses, and, in the last season of his career, even the crippling disease that ultimately claimed his life, Lou Gehrig played in a total of 2,130 games. The record, which earned him the nickname "Iron Horse," stood for more than half a century. It also defined Gehrig's career as few records have shaped the life of any other professional athlete.

When he began the 1939 season with a .143 batting average, Gehrig knew that he had to bench himself "for the good of the team."[8] Never had there been a more selfless player, or one more dedicated than he was to the Yankees. Two years later, the Iron Horse lost his battle with ALS.

Since that time Lou Gehrig has been the subject of more than a dozen biographies and two films: *Pride of the Yankees* (1942), starring Gary Cooper; and *A Love Affair: The Eleanor and Lou Gehrig Story* (1974), starring Blythe Danner and Edward Herrmann.[9] In each treatment, Gehrig emerges as a genuine American hero, a man who rose from poverty to fame, conducted his life with grace and humility, and faced an untimely death with the same quiet courage that characterized his remarkable playing career. To be sure, Gehrig's apotheosis from an exceptionally talented professional athlete to an American legend was carefully cultivated by his wife, Eleanor, after his death. But baseball was also eager to support her cause to promote the more intangible American values of honest, hard work, fair play, and personal integrity that have long been associated with the game and the heroes who have helped make it the national pastime.

*Lou Gehrig: A Biography* was written during the 100th anniversary of the Yankee slugger's birth. The book offers a fresh look at one of baseball's greatest and most beloved stars and goes beyond previous biographies by exploring the careful cultivation of the Iron Horse's legend and legacy that continue more than sixty years after his death. In telling this story, I relied on the personal correspondence of Eleanor Gehrig, newspaper accounts, and previously published biographies. I was also the beneficiary of valuable assistance from George Pollack, executor of the Gehrig estate; Ray Robinson, the author of *Iron Horse: Lou Gehrig in His Time*; Dave Kindred of the *Sporting News*; the staff at the National Baseball Hall of Fame and Library; Dorine Gordon of the National ALS Association; and John Maroon of Ripken Baseball Incorporated. Special thanks are due to Evelyn Davies, Dr. Stuart Glassman, Cal Ripken, Mike Schmidt, Jeff Silverman, and Teresa Wright for sharing their insights on the legend and legacy of Lou Gehrig, and to Bill Burdick of the Hall of Fame and Steve Gietschier of the *Sporting News* for their assistance in securing photographs and the permission to reprint them. My grandfathers, the men to whom this book is dedicated, are also owed a personal debt of gratitude. They were contemporaries of Lou Gehrig, men who shared his moral code. Although I only had the opportunity as a child to know one of them, I am told that I inherited their passion for baseball, personal character, and work ethic, qualities for which I am eternally grateful.

Finally, special thanks are due to my family—my wife Jackie and our sons Tim, Peter, and Ben—for indulging my twin passions of writing and baseball and still offering their unconditional love and support.

## NOTES

1. Ray Robinson, *Iron Horse: Lou Gehrig in His Time* (New York: W.W. Norton, 1990), 262–263.
2. "Lou Gehrig's Farewell Speech," quoted in *New York Times*, July 5, 1939.
3. Ibid.
4. Robinson, *Iron Horse*, 258–259.
5. Ibid., 264.
6. Rick Wolff, *The Baseball Encyclopedia*, 8th ed. (New York: Macmillan, 1990), 936; Mike Shatzkin, *The Ballplayers: Baseball's Ultimate Biographical Reference* (New York: William Morrow, 1990), 381–383; Ron Smith, *Baseball's Greatest Players. A Celebration of the 20th Century's Best* (St. Louis, MO: The Sporting News, 1998), 21; Mark Vancil and Peter Hirdt, eds., *Baseball's All Century Team* (Chicago: Rare Air Media, 1999), 108–111.
7. Gehrig quoted in Donald Honig, *The Power Hitters* (St. Louis, MO: The Sporting News, 1989), 35.
8. Gehrig quoted in Robinson, *Iron Horse*, 252.

9. Biographical treatments of Lou Gehrig include: Richard Bak, *Lou Gehrig: An American Classic* (Dallas, TX: Taylor Publishing, 1995); Stanley W. Carlson, *Lou Gehrig: Baseball's Iron Man* (Minneapolis, MN: S.W. Carlson, 1941); Guy Curato, *Batting 1000—Baseball's Leading Hitters: A Tribute to Lou Gehrig* (Chicago: Adams Press, 1987); Paul Gallico, *Lou Gehrig: Pride of the Yankees* (New York: Grosset & Dunlap, 1942); Eleanor Gehrig and Joseph Durso, *My Luke and I* (New York: Thomas Y. Crowell, 1976); Frank Graham, *Lou Gehrig: A Quiet Hero* (New York: G.P. Putnam's Sons, 1942); Richard Hubler, *Lou Gehrig: Iron Horse of Baseball* (Boston: Houghton Mifflin, 1941); and Ray Robinson, *Iron Horse: Lou Gehrig in His Time* (New York: W.W. Norton, 1990). There are also several children's biographies, including: David A. Adler, *Lou Gehrig: The Luckiest Man* (San Diego: Harcourt Brace, 1997); Keith Brandt, *Lou Gehrig: Pride of the Yankees* (Mahwah, NJ: Troll Associates, 1986); Willard Luce and Celia Luce, *Lou Gehrig: Iron Man of Baseball* (Champaign, IL: Garrard, 1970); Norman L. Macht, *Baseball Legends: Lou Gehrig* (New York: Chelsea House, 1993); Richard Rambeck, *Lou Gehrig* (Mankato, MN: Child's World, 1994); Robert Rubin, *Lou Gehrig: Courageous Star* (New York: Putnam, 1979); and Guernsey Van Riper, *Lou Gehrig: Boy of the Sandlots* (Indianapolis, IN: Bobbs-Merrill, Inc., 1949).

In 1917, 14-year-old Lou Gehrig poses in a studio with his grade-school diploma. *National Baseball Hall of Fame Library, Cooperstown, N.Y.*

# Born and Bred in New York City, 1903–1920

When Heinrich Ludwig Gehrig arrived in New York City at the dawn of the twentieth century, he hoped to find employment as an art metal mechanic. Emigrating to the United States from Baden, Germany, in 1888, the 21-year-old artisan initially settled in Chicago.[1] But with few prospects for employment he decided to relocate to the more affluent Empire City where his unique skill of hammering intricate designs into sheet metal would almost certainly be in demand. What he discovered was a metropolis of 3.4 million residents spread across five boroughs, connected by a network of bridges, streetcars, and ferryboats.[2] While New York's population was second only to London, the city's wealth was not as evenly distributed as Gehrig had imagined.

To be sure, New York was the uncontested economic capital of the United States, being home to the stock exchange, investment banks, brokerage houses, businesses, and shipping interests that fueled the industrial revolution. But the wealth of the city was concentrated on the Upper East Side of Manhattan where Wall Street propelled the wheels of commerce and provided a lucrative playground for such robber barons as J. P. Morgan, August Belmont, and Jacob Schiff. The nation's most powerful corporations operated out of the high-rise office buildings that dominated the skyline. Department stores such as Wanamaker's, Macy's, Altman's, Siegal Cooper, and Lord & Taylor composed the renown shopping district known as the "Ladies Mile," which ran from 8th Street to 23rd Street, bounded by Broadway to the east and 6th Avenue to the west.[3] Fashionable nightclubs, opulent theaters, and federal-style opera houses could also be found on the Upper East Side, giving the city a well-deserved reputation as the entertainment capital of the nation. But there was also another, less attractive New York.

The "other" New York was concentrated on Manhattan's Lower East Side, the gateway to the "American Dream" for European immigrants. Skilled and unskilled, they came by the thousands from Germany, Italy, Austria-Hungary, and Russia. Most were dirt poor and lived from hand to mouth, eking out a meager existence by working long hours in the area's factories and sweatshops. Crowding into filthy, dimly lit tenement buildings, the newcomers struggled with insufferable living conditions. The five- and six-story tenements were situated on 25-foot by 100-foot lots and inhabited by twenty or more families. Overcrowding was due, in part, to those immigrants who took in boarders to help pay the $10-a-month rent. Some of the older tenements, built in the mid-nineteenth century, had no toilets or running water. Only one room in each apartment received direct light or ventilation. The others were small 8-foot by 6-foot cubicles completely devoid of any fresh air or natural light and were shared by rats, mice, and roaches. The basements of these buildings often housed makeshift saloons and brothels and thus were breeding grounds for crime and vice.[4] Not until 1901, when progressive reformers lobbied the state legislature for a new Tenement House Law, were these dismal conditions addressed.[5]

Gehrig was one of approximately 210,000 German immigrants who came to New York at the turn of the century to better his future.[6] Many of these immigrants settled in Kleindeutschland, or "Little Germany," which was among the earliest of the Lower East Side's ethnic enclaves established in the 1840s.[7] The most ambitious arrivals pooled their resources so that they could eventually relocate to the lower middle-class neighborhoods of Yorkville, Harlem, Brooklyn, Queens, and the Bronx.[8] Although Gehrig was not the most enterprising individual, preferring to spend his time in the local tavern rather than working at his trade, he had no intention of starting his new life on the Lower East Side.[9] Instead, he saved enough money to pay the $20-a-month rent for a small apartment in Yorkville and settled into a modest but comfortable lifestyle.[10]

In 1899, Gehrig met Christina Flack, a recent immigrant from the German province of Schleswig-Holstein, near the Danish border. She was fourteen years younger than Heinrich and, at 6 feet, 200 pounds, the blond-haired, blue-eyed Christina presented a striking, if not formidable, appearance. Her genial disposition and deference won Heinrich's affections and the couple was married on November 27, 1900.[11]

Life was hard for the Gehrigs. Because Heinrich seldom enjoyed steady employment, Christina felt obligated to accept as much work as possible cleaning the houses and washing the laundry of Manhattan's wealthier families. The couple moved often and lived in cramped apartments with few conveniences. But they remained in Yorkville because the German-American community there offered some semblance of security in their new homeland. Neighbors spoke their native language, read German newspapers, and attended the Lutheran Church.[12] German culture was also transplanted in the fraternal and mutual aid societies, in the sports clubs, and in the turnverein, a combination social club, debating society, and gymnasium where a young man could cultivate his mind through intellectual discussion and his body through calisthenics.[13] If Yorkville alleviated the cultural insecurity the Gehrigs felt over being accepted by the American mainstream, their attitude changed once they tried to have children.

Tenements were known to breed contagious illnesses like diphtheria, tuberculosis, and cholera, and infant mortality rates were especially high among newborns exposed to such congested living conditions. Of the four children born to Christina and Heinrich Gehrig, only one survived past infancy. Anna, born in 1902, died of an unknown illness a year later. Another daughter, Sophie, was born in 1904 and succumbed to diphtheria within the year. A son died so soon after his birth that he was never given a name. Christina became more grief-stricken with the death of each one. Only her second child, a son born on June 19, 1903, would live to see childhood. Named Henry Louis Gehrig after his father, Lou, as he came to be known, was a healthy boy who weighed almost 14 pounds at birth.[14] "He's the only big egg I have in my basket," Christina would later say of the child, who became the sole object of her affections. "He's the only one of the four who lived, so I want him to have the best."[15] She remained true to her word.

At the time of Lou's birth, the Gehrigs lived in a tenement house at 94th Street in Yorkville.[16] Intent on escaping their congested living conditions, the family relocated to Washington Heights when their son was 5 years old. Their new neighborhood at 179th Street and Amsterdam Avenue was not much better, but it did have more open space and fresh air than Yorkville. The Gehrigs managed to settle into a hectic but modestly comfortable life. Lou attended P.S. 132 at 183rd Street and Wadsworth Avenue, where he learned to read, write, and speak English. After school, he contributed to the family's income by picking up and delivering the laundry his mother washed and by running errands in the neighborhood.[17] While Heinrich spent more time drinking and playing pinochle at the local tavern than plying his trade, Christina continued to work as a domestic and assumed the primary responsibility for raising Lou. Years later she proudly claimed that her son "never left the table hungry" and that he was "always clean and neatly dressed" when she sent him off to grade school.[18] Given the couple's financial tensions, the household was not a happy one, and the stress often resulted in loud, heated arguments delivered in a hybrid of broken English and German.[19]

Heinrich took little interest in his son's upbringing. According to Paul Gallico, Gehrig's first biographer, Pop Gehrig was more of a disciplinarian whose heavy hand only served to intimidate his son. As a result, Lou developed a low sense of self-esteem, which he struggled to overcome for the remainder of his life.[20] "I was a pretty bad kid," he said in a 1930 interview. "I was raised in the city streets and did not miss a single trick. I played ball and marbles and spent as much time as possible in the Hudson River."[21] Compared to street corner toughs whose activities bordered on the criminal, Gehrig was exaggerating his own case. If he ran with a gang, they were a social bunch, concerned chiefly with playing sports. His friends were Irish, Hungarian, and German kids who woke up at 5:00 A.M. to play soccer, football, or baseball in the streets until it was time for school.[22] The most mischief they created was going skinny dipping off an old coal barge in the Harlem River, a stunt for which they were arrested. After Pop Gehrig posted bail for his son, Lou received such a severe spanking that he never dared to risk a similar adventure.[23] Instead, he began to develop a passionate interest in baseball.

Since Washington Heights was the home of the American League's New York Highlanders, the predecessors of the mighty Yankees, youngsters often spent their summer afternoons at Hilltop Park. Located on the west side of Broadway, between West 165th and 168th Streets, Hilltop sat on Manhattan's highest elevation and afforded spectators a scenic view of the Hudson River and the New Jersey Palisades. The ballpark had a roofed single-decked wooden grandstand that hugged the infield. Open single-decked bleachers continued down the foul lines to the outfield fences. Kids who couldn't afford to pay admission formed a knothole gang outside the 20-foot-high fences paralleling Broadway and 168th Street.[24]

Despite their convenient location, Lou's favorite team was not the Highlanders but the National League's Giants.[25] Managed by the fiery John McGraw, the team captured the loyalties of New Yorkers by fielding consistent winners. During the first quarter of the twentieth century, the Giants, featuring such star performers as Christy Mathewson, Frankie Frisch, and Mel Ott, won ten pennants and three world championships (1905, 1921, 1922). The Highlanders, on the other hand, didn't capture a single flag during their years in Washington Heights. Their glory years wouldn't arrive until 1920 when George Herman Ruth would propell them into the national spotlight with his remarkable power hitting.

To be sure, young Lou had plenty of baseball heroes. Like most youngsters, he collected cigarette cards of Ruth, Mathewson, Ty Cobb, and Tris Speaker.

But his favorite player was Honus Wagner, the hard-hitting shortstop of the Pittsburgh Pirates. Not only was Wagner a German-American, but his behavior reflected the modesty and decorum that Lou admired.[26] Lou, like most other hyphenated Americans, developed a life-long fascination with a game that was quickly becoming the national pastime.

Baseball was a symbolic representation of the heart and mind of the American national character because it promised each individual the opportunity to step up to the plate and get his chance for glory. Sportswriters often identified the game with values of democracy and fair play, suggesting that it was an important vehicle in the assimilation process because it cut across the ethnic and socioeconomic barriers that divided immigrants from others not of their own ethnicity. Regardless of his religious or ethnic background, the baseball player competed on even terms with his opponents and, in the process, crystallized the "rags-to-riches" success story that became so cherished among the first generation of European immigrants.

"Baseball is our real melting pot," wrote Frederick Lieb, president of the National Baseball Writers' Association. "Next to the little red school house, there has been no greater agency in bringing together our different races than our national game."[27] The sons of immigrants were even more secure in their American identity and chose to play baseball because it was *their* pastime. They grew up with the game in the streets, in school, and in the newspapers. It was a rite of passage for them. Some of the parents, however, did not share their sons' enthusiasm for the sport.

Mom and Pop Gehrig thought baseball was a waste of time and worried that their son would become a "bummer" if he continued to indulge in it.[28] Their skepticism was due, in part, to their ignorance of the game, and the association they made between it and the street corner gangs who often played stickball. "Mom Gehrig had no conception of baseball, none whatsoever," recalled David Blumenthal, one of Lou's childhood friends. "She once invited me to dinner and questioned me about the game. She thought it was played on the streets. She had no idea that it was played in a stadium."[29]

Of course, Lou was not as streetwise as other urban kids. He was a very shy, sensitive youngster whose feelings were easily hurt. Even as an adult, the childhood memory of killing a bird brought tears to his eyes. "When I was a kid I went out bird shooting with some friends," he once told a Yankee teammate who had asked him to go hunting. "I shot a bird and after I saw it lying on the ground dead, I felt so badly I cried. I dug a grave for it and buried it there, and swore I'd never go hunting again."[30]

Lou also possessed an unusually mature respect for authority, which prevented him from playing hooky or missing a single day through eight years of grade school, even when he was ill.[31] His need to behave properly also reflected a strong desire to please his mother, whom he not only loved but revered. Lou was a classic mama's boy who was physically big for his age. His reserved disposition, awkward manner, and German heritage made him an easy target for preadolescent ridicule, especially after the outbreak of World War I in Europe during the summer of 1914.

As a virulent anti-German hysteria swept the nation, German-Americans suffered verbal harassment and sometimes physical assault. Matters only worsened after the United States declared war on Germany in April 1917. German organizations came under attack as their newspapers were shut down and their property destroyed.[32] Like other German-Americans, Lou was forced to endure the taunts of other kids who berated him as "Heinie," "dumb Dutchman," and "Krauthead."[33] It was during this same time that Pop Gehrig overheard one of his son's friends jokingly describe Lou as "all belly and ass." Whether that particular insult or a combination of all the other nativist slurs directed at his son evoked the father's sympathy is not certain. But what is known is that Pop Gehrig began sending his 12-year-old boy to a Yorkville turnverein to burn off the excess weight, improve his coordination, and tone his muscles. Lou worked so diligently at building his body that by age 16 he possessed a well-defined physique and one that commanded the attention and respect of his peers.[34] Not only did he develop the impressive work ethic that became his trademark as a professional baseball player in later years, but he also began to find his niche in life.

Lou graduated from elementary school in June 1917. Since Pop Gehrig became ill a few months earlier, he could no longer be counted on for the meager earnings he contributed to the family's income. When Lou offered to forgo high school to take a job, Christina refused her permission. Like many ambitious immigrants, she realized that education was the key to upward mobility and hoped that her son would eventually attend college to study architecture or engineering.[35] Accordingly, Lou, at the insistence of his mother, entered Commerce High School, an all-boys secondary school that prepared students for employment in the business world. While the curriculum was devoted to bookkeeping, typing, and clerical work, and few of the graduates matriculated to college, Commerce did provide students with the basic communications skills necessary for undergraduate training.[36]

Each morning Lou woke up early, readied himself for the day, and took the subway to 155 West 65th Street where Commerce was located. After school, the stocky adolescent earned money by taking odd jobs at grocery stores and butcher shops and by delivering newspapers.[37] This busy schedule did not allow him to participate in after-school sports, the quickest way to meet and make new friends. Already shy by nature, Lou was a loner during his first year at Commerce. Arthur Narins, a classmate, recalled that Gehrig was a "poor boy" who "came to school on cold winter days wearing no overcoat or hat."[38] Oliver Gintel, another classmate, asked Lou to try out for the soccer team, but the shy youngster refused, insisting that "he wasn't good at athletics" and that his "mother wouldn't give her permission." "Lou was criticized for his utter lack of school spirit," said Gintel, "and was being called a 'sissy' and a 'Mamma's Boy.' Always smiling, he paid no attention to any of the criticisms and minded his own business."[39] But Gintel and others recognized Lou's exceptional athletic ability in pick-up games and enlisted the support of a teacher to recruit him. "Some of the kids told my bookkeeping teacher that I could hit the ball a mile," Lou recalled in an interview, years later. "The teacher ordered me to show up for a school game. When I got to the stadium and saw so many people going in and heard all the cheering and noise, I was so scared that I couldn't see straight. I turned around, got back on the street car, and went home. The next day the teacher threatened to flunk me if I didn't show up for the next game. So I went."[40]

Gehrig quickly became a three-sport athlete in high school, competing in football, baseball, and soccer. Of the three sports, he excelled at soccer, leading Commerce to three straight interscholastic championships in 1919, 1920, and 1921. On the gridiron, he proved to be a star fullback whose most impressive feat came in the fall of 1920 when he threw a 40-yard forward pass against Brooklyn's Commerce High School to clinch a 9–6 victory.[41] Ironically, Lou's weakest sport was baseball. During his first season on the team he hit an anemic .150 and performed just adequately at first base and in the outfield.[42] But he loved the game and worked extremely hard to improve his performance. According to Harry Kane, the Commerce baseball coach, Lou was "the greatest athlete I ever coached. He constantly wanted to learn. When a weakness cropped up in his play he worked hard to eradicate it. For instance, his main weakness in baseball was his inability to hit left-handed curve ball pitching. We set to work together, and after a few weeks of practice, day in and day out, he completely overcame his fault."[43] By the end of his second year on the team, Lou was hitting .300 and, according to one teacher, could "hit a baseball without missing a stroke."[44] Lou spent that summer working odd jobs and, on Sundays, pitching for local semi-pro teams, who would pay him $5 a game.[45]

In the spring of 1920, Commerce's baseball team was selected by the *New York Daily News* to represent the city in a championship game against Chicago's best scholastic team, Lane Technical High School, in the Windy City. When Lou, a strapping 6-foot, 185-pound junior who pitched and played first base, asked his parents for permission to travel to Chicago, they promptly refused to give it. Kane intervened, promising that he would assume personal responsibility for their son. Grudgingly, they agreed to let their son go.

The trip proved to be an adventure of "firsts" for Lou: the first time away from home, the first train ride, the first time meeting a U.S. president (William Howard Taft, then a Supreme Court justice and a former president, traveled on the same train and offered his best wishes to the team), and the first appearance in a major league baseball park.[46] The game was played on June 26 at Wrigley Field before a crowd of 10,000 spectators. Gehrig played first base and hit third. Eli Jacobs, Commerce's best pitcher, started the game, but surrendered four runs in the first inning. He eventually settled down, surrendering only two more runs over the next seven innings. Gehrig went hitless until the ninth. With Commerce already ahead 8–6, Lou went to bat with the bases loaded. After taking the first pitch, he knocked the second offering over the right-field fence onto Sheffield Avenue for a grand slam. The blow increased Commerce's margin of victory by four runs, 12–6.[47]

Gehrig's blast was so impressive that sportswriters dubbed him the "Babe Ruth of the school yards."[48] It was a reflection of better things to come. In three short years, Lou would be Ruth's teammate on the New York Yankees. Together, they would form the most prodigious power-hitting combination in the history of the national pastime.

## NOTES

1. Ray Robinson, *Iron Horse: Lou Gehrig and His Time* (New York: Oxford University Press, 1990), 30.

2. See Allon Schoener, *New York: An Illustrated History of the People* (New York: W.W. Norton, 1998), 108. Schoener lists New York City's population in 1898 as 3.36 million.

3. Kenneth T. Jackson and David S. Dunbar, eds., *Empire City: New York through the Centuries* (New York: Columbia University Press, 2002), 400.

4. Ibid., 430; Ruth Limmer and Andrew S. Dolkart, "The Tenement as History and Housing," Lower East Side Tenement Museum Web site, 2001, http://www.tenement.org; and Selma Berrol, *The Empire City: New York and Its People, 1624–1996* (Westport, CT: Praeger, 1997), 75, 94–95.

5. Jackson and Dunbar, *Empire City*, 399–400, 422.

6. Schoener, *New York*, 144. Between 1880 and 1889, 1,445,181 Germans immigrated to the United States. By 1900, there were 750,000 Germans living in New York City, and of that number 210,723 were foreign-born.

7. Ibid.

8. Ibid., 145.

9. Richard Bak, *Lou Gehrig: An American Classic* (Dallas, TX: Taylor Publishing, 1995), 9.

10. Ibid., 3.

11. Robinson, *Iron Horse*, 30–31.

12. See Oscar Handlin, *The Uprooted*, 2nd ed. (Boston: Little, Brown & Co., 1973), 153–165. Handlin identifies an important dialectic in the assimilation process of all immigrant groups. On one hand, they tried to navigate nativist hostility by learning English, encouraging their children to adopt American customs, and establishing mutual aid societies. On the other hand, immigrants tended to live among those of their own ethnicity, transplant native institutions in these ethnic enclaves, and continue to speak their native language, thereby alienating themselves from the American mainstream.

13. Larry R. Gerlach, "German Americans in Major League Baseball: Sport and Acculturation," in *The American Game: Baseball and Ethnicity*, eds. Lawrence Baldassaro and Richard A. Johnson (Carbondale, IL: Southern Illinois University Press, 2002), 27.

14. Bak, *American Classic*, 3.

15. Christina Gehrig quoted in Robinson, *Iron Horse*, 32.

16. Eleanor Gehrig and Joseph Durso, *My Luke and I* (New York: Thomas Y. Crowell, 1976), 30.

17. Bak, *American Classic*, 10.

18. Christina Gehrig quoted in Bak, *American Classic*, 9.

19. Gehrig and Durso, *My Luke and I*, 30.

20. Paul Gallico, *Lou Gehrig: Pride of the Yankees* (New York: Grosset & Dunlap, 1942) 38.

21. Lou Gehrig quoted in Harry T. Bundidge, "Gehrig Gives Baseball Full Credit for Rescuing Parents and Self from New York Tenement District," *Sporting News*, December 25, 1930.

22. Gehrig and Durso, *My Luke and I*, 32.

23. Gallico, *Pride of the Yankees*, 39.

24. Lawrence S. Ritter, *Lost Ballparks: A Celebration of Baseball's Legendary Fields* (New York: Viking Studio Books, 1992), 91–93.

25. Gehrig and Durso, *My Luke and I*, 34.

26. Ibid.; and Gerlach, "German Americans in Baseball," 32–33.

27. Frederick G. Lieb, "Baseball—The Nation's Melting Pot," *Baseball Magazine*, August 1923, 393–394.

28. Christina Gehrig quoted in Robinson, *Iron Horse*, 34. According to historian G. Edward White, German-Americans, unlike most other immigrant groups, assimilated more quickly into the American mainstream because of their enterprising nature, job skills, and emphasis on education. Under these circumstances, baseball was not viewed by them as a means of social mobility as much as a way to make money, especially after the 1880s when the game was transformed from amateur recreation to commercial entertainment. See G. Edward White, *Creating the National Pastime: Baseball Transforms Itself, 1903–1953* (Princeton, NJ: Princeton University Press, 1996), 245–274.

29. David Blumenthal quoted in ESPN Classics Video, *Sports Century: Lou Gehrig*, 2000.

30. Lou Gehrig to Bill Dickey quoted in Gallico, *Pride of the Yankees*, 10.

31. Gehrig and Durso, *My Luke and I*, 36.

32. See Frederick C. Luebke, *Bonds of Loyalty: German-Americans and World War I* (DeKalb, IL: Northern Illinois University Press, 1974).

33. Gerlach, "German Americans in Baseball," 44.

34. Bak, *American Classic*, 11–12; and Robinson, *Iron Horse*, 37. According to Ray Robinson, the "belly and ass" remark came from one of Lou's best friends, Mike Sesit. The two worked out together at the Yorkville turnverein and, afterwards, indulged themselves with pastries at the local German coffee shops.

35. Bak, *American Classic*, 17.

36. Robinson, *Iron Horse*, 34.

37. Ibid.; Bak, *American Classic*, 18; and Gallico, *Pride of the Yankees*, 48.

38. Arthur Narins quoted in Gallico, *Pride of the Yankees*, 43.

39. Oliver Gintel quoted in ibid., 43–44.

40. Lou Gehrig quoted in Stanley Frank, "Gehrig Ran Out on First Game," *New York Post*, August 7, 1934.

41. Frank Graham, *Lou Gehrig: A Quiet Hero* (New York: G.P. Putnam's Sons, 1942), 11.

42. Ibid.; and Gallico, *Pride of the Yankees*, 45.

43. Harry Kane quoted in Graham, *Quiet Hero*, 22–23.

44. Gallico, *Pride of the Yankees*, 45; and Mollie Silverman quoted in Robinson, *Iron Horse*, 39.

45. Gallico, *Pride of the Yankees*, 49; and Gehrig and Durso, *My Luke and I*, 39.

46. Bak, *American Classic*, 20; and Gehrig and Durso, *My Luke and I*, 40.

47. Robinson, *Iron Horse*, 42–43.

48. Bak, *American Classic*, 20–21; Robinson, *Iron Horse*, 42–43. Frank Graham, one of Gehrig's first biographers, credits Gehrig with a game-winning grand slam. See *Quiet Hero*, 16–18.

# Columbia Days, 1921–1923

During Lou's final year at Commerce High School, his mother Christina found steady work for her family at Columbia University's Phi Delta Theta fraternity house. While she cooked and cleaned, Pop Gehrig, recovered from his illness, served as a handyman and janitor, and Lou waited on tables after school.[1] He somehow managed to make it back into the city for work each evening from Commerce's practice field at a Catholic seminary in the east Bronx.[2]

Christina entertained dreams of her son's matriculating to Columbia to study architecture or engineering, two professions at which German-Americans excelled, but Columbia was well beyond the financial means of the Gehrig family. Not until Lou captured the interest of the university's football coach, Frank "Buck" O'Neill, did a college education become possible.

During the fall of 1920, Robert Watt, Columbia's graduate manager of athletics, gave his permission for Commerce High School to play its arch rival, DeWitt Clinton, at the university's South Field. Not only would the contest promote good relations between the university and the city's high schools, but it would also serve as a recruiting mechanism to attract the most outstanding school boy athletes to Columbia. On game day, Watt sat in the bleachers with O'Neill perusing the field for prospective football players. Both men were impressed by Lou's performance at half back and, afterwards, offered him an athletic scholarship to Columbia.[3] Because Commerce did not offer a college preparatory program, however, Lou had to enter Columbia's extension department to earn enough credits so that he could enroll in the fall as a full-time freshman. His scholarship was contingent on successfully completing the coursework.[4]

"Columbia Lou" in 1923, his only season with the Columbia University Lions baseball team. *National Baseball Hall of Fame Library, Cooperstown, N.Y.*

Gehrig graduated from Commerce in February, 1921 and began his studies in the university's extension program. Andy Coakley, Columbia's baseball coach, gave Lou permission to work out with the baseball team during the spring practice sessions, although he was not allowed to play in any games. The only exception was an April 5th exhibition contest against the Hartford Senators of the Eastern League. Gehrig hit a pair of long home runs in the game, capturing the interest of Art Devlin, a scout for the New York Giants.[5] Devlin courted Gehrig, convincing him that he could retain his amateur status and play for pay with Hartford, which had a working arrangement with John McGraw's New York Giants. He also promised the impressionable youth a tryout at the Polo Grounds before McGraw himself.[6] Lou couldn't resist the offer. Not only would he be able to contribute to his family's income, but he would also get to meet one of his boyhood idols.

Lou reported to the Polo Grounds where he put on a magnificent display of power hitting. But after taking the field, he misplayed a routine ground ball at first and McGraw dismissed him as "just another lousy ballplayer." Gehrig was hurt by the rebuff and would hold it against McGraw for the rest of his life.[7] Nevertheless, Lou agreed to join the Hartford club and, on June 3, made his professional debut against the Pittsfield Hillies under the assumed name of "Lou Lewis." Gehrig played the entire game at first base, but went hitless in three at-bats in the 2–1 Hartford victory. He recorded his first hit—a triple—the following day against Waterbury in another Hartford win, this one by a score of 5–3. Lou collected four more hits during the next four games, three for extra bases, and was hitting at a .261 clip.[8] Although Lou didn't hit any home runs, the *Hartford Times* acknowledged that the "young first sacker is a slugger whose present work gives hope that he will add to Hartford's pennant-winning chain."[9]

When Coakley discovered that his first base prospect was playing pro ball in violation of Columbia's athletic policy, he traveled to Hartford to inform Lou that he had jeopardized his scholarship.[10] Gehrig immediately left the team and returned to New York. Watt informed the Columbia Athletic Council of the violation, urging members not to be too severe in its punishment. Stating his belief that Gehrig made an innocent mistake, Watt suggested a compromise solution: bar Lou from intercollegiate competition in both football and baseball during his freshman year, which was to start that September, but allow him to compete beginning in the fall of 1922. After informing Columbia's athletic rivals of the violation and receiving their consent to reinstate Gehrig after one year of ineligibility, the Council agreed to the compromise. Lou would be reinstated for his sophomore year. Until then, he would only be allowed to practice with the football and baseball teams.[11]

The decision reflected the delicate balance between ethics and competition stressed by the faculty committee that controlled Columbia's athletic program during the early twentieth century. Unlike other collegiate sports programs that emphasized winning and fund-raising to placate their alumni and trustees, Columbia strove to "win ethically while staying solvent." Although the university's Athletic Council understood that putting a consistent winner on the field kept the turnstiles spinning and the athletic program out of debt, it stressed the paramount importance of ethical competition, especially in the high-profile sport of football.[12] In fact, the football program had been abolished at the college in 1905 because of the faculty's concern about its negative impact on the quality of student work and the academic reputation of the institution.[13] Football returned to Columbia in 1915, and by the 1920s the sport was an integral part of the social life on campus. Students placed a greater emphasis on extracurricular activities, defining their place in the fraternity and on the athletic field. Those who had the talent to compete were most popular; those who didn't had a responsibility to demonstrate school spirit by attending the games and cheering on their more athletically inclined fraternity brothers. Such allegiance was a fundamental part of the peer culture that was developing on college campuses in the 1920s, and football was a major vehicle for promoting it.[14]

Columbia, in spite of the faculty's emphasis on academic achievement and ethical competition, was under tremendous pressure by both students and alumni to produce winning football teams. Buck O'Neill was hired to achieve that goal.[15] In 1922, he built Columbia's backfield around Gehrig and Wally Koppisch, a future All-American. The duo performed exceptionally well during the first four games, leading the Lions to a perfect 4–0 record. In the opener against Ursinus College, Koppisch ran for three touchdowns and Lou scored two, as Columbia shellacked the small Pennsylvania school, 30–0. Amherst was also humbled by the Gehrig-Koppisch tandem, 43–6. The next two contests were closer but the Lions prevailed, defeating Wesleyan, 10–6, and New York University, 7–6. Again, the difference proved to be the Gehrig-Koppisch backfield. After that, Columbia's season took a turn for the worse, as the Lions suffered defeats against Williams (13–10), Cornell (56–0), Darmouth (28–7), and Colgate (59–6). The team's last victory came against Middlebury, 17–6, to finish the season with a 5–4 record.[16]

It would be the one and only football season that Gehrig played for Columbia. If nothing else, some of the more lopsided defeats taught him never to take his athletic successes for granted. "He was a battler," said Robert Pulleyn, one of Lou's teammates on the 1922 squad. "On the football field Lou worked with everything he had."[17] He was also a team player, agreeing to play wherever

O'Neill needed him, including the offensive and defensive lines.[18] Despite his success on the gridiron, Lou was never fully accepted by his peers because of his more modest origins and unsophisticated manner.

Contrary to popular belief, the college-going youth of the 1920s were not "rebellious, frivolous and lost to social responsibility and traditional values." As children of the white middle class, they were socially and economically secure and enjoyed the luxuries of a higher education and considerable leisure time compared to previous generations. But they also recognized that "individual merit came from group strength; that personal identity resulted from rigid conformity; and that social stratification bred the kind of community homogeneity" that their parents valued.[19] Accordingly, the college-going youth of the 1920s adopted the fraternity as the main engine of social control in their quest for conformity. At Columbia, fraternities were at their peak in terms of numbers and influence. The university had thirty-six fraternity houses by 1923 and each one had its own set of codes, standards, and values.[20] Personal conformity to those standards, whether they be in drinking, dress, or sexual conventions, was a demonstration of the individual's loyalty to the fraternity and its members. "Registration in the University presumes a certain subjective attitude towards the traditions," wrote the editor of the *Columbia Spectator.* "If a man cannot take part in those customs he can at least conform. No university is required to continue on its rolls any man or group of men who frankly show that they are using its educational facilities in a purely selfish way."[21] Accordingly, those most admired on campus were the "compromise types" who were "willing to subordinate personal interest to group needs."[22]

Gehrig's shyness and inability to navigate the social customs of the fraternity would have made him an outcast had it not been for his athletic prowess. Perhaps the only reason he was made a member of the Phi Delta fraternity was because of his family's employment there and because of his own gridiron exploits, which brought greater prestige to the fraternity.[23] Even then, Lou was humiliated by Phi Delta's rushing period, when prospective candidates are tested for membership, and he was often the target of "razzing" by members bent on shaming him into conformity with their preferences for clothing, music, and dating habits.[24] To make matters worse, much of their petty sarcasm came while he was waiting on their dinner tables. Yet the only reference Gehrig ever made of their cruelty was a dismissive admission to sportswriter Paul Gallico that his fraternity brothers "weren't very nice" to him and that he "never felt as if [he] belonged to the college" because of it.[25]

At 6 feet, 200 pounds, Gehrig was a stunningly handsome young man with wavy brown hair, dimpled cheeks, and a muscular physique. Many of the female students at Barnard, Columbia's sister campus, were attracted by his looks as well as his athletic ability. But they quickly lost interest when they saw him off the field in his worn clothes, or discovered that his mother was a fraternity house cook. He lacked the social graces and wealth that these young women valued. Those who did approach Gehrig found that his introverted disposition made him rather awkward in their company, discouraging any notions of a dating relationship.[26] On the other hand, Lou was too much of a gentleman to engage in the casual sexual activity that had become an acceptable part of peer culture in the 1920s.[27] Ultimately, Gehrig's disillusioning experience with campus culture only served to increase his self-consciousness, forcing him to withdraw even further from his peers. Where he did excel was on the baseball diamond.

Baseball did not enjoy the same popularity as football at Columbia. Major league clubs relied primarily on the minor leagues to develop talent, not the colleges. Still, Columbia enjoyed a unique history with the sport, beginning in 1858 when it played its first interscholastic game against the Columbia Academy, a college preparatory school. By 1867, the college had created a $200 budget for the specific purpose of purchasing baseball equipment.[28] In 1914, Columbia hired Andy Coakley, an outstanding pitcher at Holy Cross College who later starred for Connie Mack's Philadelphia Athletics.[29] Coakley enjoyed a thirty-eight-year tenure as the university's baseball coach but few championships.[30] Nevertheless, Gehrig credited Coakley with much of his own professional success, especially for teaching Lou how to hit the curve ball.[31]

When Lou wasn't playing first base for the Lions, he pitched or played the outfield. "Lou was a fair outfielder, a first baseman without any glaring weakness, and a good pitcher," said Coakley when asked to evaluate Gehrig's talent. "In the outfield he covered a lot of ground, got most of the drives hit his way, and got the ball away fast with a strong arm. As a pitcher, he didn't have much stuff, but he did have a better fastball than most college pitchers. Some days no college team could beat him."[32] On other days, he couldn't seem to win in spite of an outstanding performance. On April 18, for example, Lou pitched against Williams at Columbia's South Field. He recorded 17 strikeouts and still lost the game 5–1.[33] Gehrig's hitting was even more impressive.

His first home run of the season came on April 21, 1923, against Cornell at Ithaca, New York. It was a magnificent blow that kept rising as it cleared the right field fence. "That right field at Cornell had a high fence, then there was a road back of it, then a forest," recalled George Moeschen, the second baseman and captain of Columbia's 1923 team. "Lou lifted his home run into the forest. I looked over at Coach Coakley, sitting near me on the bench, and he was slapping his head in wonder."[34] Two days later, Columbia traveled to New Brunswick, New Jersey, to play Rutgers. On the train was Yankee scout

Paul Krichell, who approached Coakley and asked if he had any promising players. Coakley mentioned a "left-handed kid who throws pretty good and hits," but never referred to Lou by name. Since Columbia started a right-hander that day, Krichell assumed Coakley changed his plans and instead focused his attention on the team's right-fielder, a broad-shouldered youth who smashed two home runs. After the game, Krichell discovered that Coakley's right-fielder was indeed the prospect he had referred to on the train ride.[35]

Krichell returned to New York and told Yankee general manager Ed Barrow that he had discovered "another Babe Ruth." Barrow ordered his scout to follow Gehrig's progress over the next few weeks.[36] On April 28, Krichell was in the stands again, this time to watch Gehrig pitch against New York University at Columbia's South Field. Lou hurled a six-hitter, striking out eight batters. Of greater interest to Krichell though was the towering home run Gehrig hit, which cleared 116th Street and landed some 450 feet away from home plate.[37] "If he can hit major league pitching, he may be another Babe Ruth," wrote sportswriter Hugh Fullerton, echoing the same comparison that had been made two years earlier when Lou was in high school.[38] Suddenly Gehrig was the biggest star in collegiate baseball, attracting the interest of Connie Mack, who was building another championship dynasty in Philadelphia.

Mack, who favored college-educated players, learned of "Columbia Lou" from Eddie Collins, an earlier Columbia product who was the second baseman for the Philadelphia Athletics' first championship dynasty in 1910–1914.[39] Lou's performance against the University of Pennsylvania confirmed Mack's decision to go after him. Facing Penn's Walter Huntzinger, widely considered to be the best college pitcher in the East, Gehrig hurled a gem. With the score tied 2–2 in the ninth, Lou won his own game with another prodigious shot.[40] Duly impressed, Mack hoped to sign Gehrig, but he was too late.[41]

On April 29, Yankee general manager Ed Barrow offered Gehrig $3,500, a price that included a $1,500 bonus, to sign with the organization. With a deep insecurity over his ability to handle the academics at Columbia and his parents' increasing medical bills, Lou accepted the Yankees' offer to the strong dismay of his mother, who did not see baseball as a legitimate profession.[42] But Lou refused to change his mind. "The financial inducement for me to leave Columbia was tremendous," he recalled years later. "Both father and mother were very ill and the money was all gone, so it was up to me to go to work. When I received an offer from the Yankees and was paid a bonus for signing a contract, I took it. That bonus bought a lot of food, paid a lot of house rent and doctor's bills. It certainly was a Godsend."[43]

When Gehrig completed his only baseball season at Columbia he had set three school records for hitting, with a .444 batting average, 7 home runs, and a .937 slugging average, and a pitching record for most strikeouts in a single game with 17.[44] "Lou is the greatest young hitter I've ever seen," said Coakley, offering his highest praise. "Though he bats left-handed, he hits equally well to all fields and is just as likely to drive one out of the park to left as he is to right."[45] The only difference was that now "Columbia Lou" would be hitting those home runs for the Yankee organization.

## NOTES

1. Gehrig and Durso, *My Luke and I,* 39; and Robinson, *Iron Horse,* 39.
2. Graham, *Quiet Hero,* 12.
3. Ibid., 20–27.
4. Gehrig and Durso, *My Luke and I,* 67.
5. Norton Chellgren, "Gehrig's Debut Was Strictly on the Sly," *Washington Times,* April 23, 1986.
6. Robinson, *Iron Horse,* 45.
7. Ibid., 46; and Charles C. Alexander, *John McGraw* (New York: Penguin, 1989), 335.
8. Bak, *American Classic,* 26.
9. Chellgren, "Gehrig's Debut Was Strictly on the Sly."
10. Robinson, *Iron Horse,* 48; and Mark Gallagher and Walter LaConte, *The Yankee Encyclopedia,* 5th ed. (New York: Sports Publishing, 2001), 101.
11. Graham, *A Quiet Hero,* 34–42. Some of Gehrig's biographers claim that Gehrig violated his amateur status again in the summer of 1922 playing for semi-pro clubs in Morristown, New Jersey, and Yonkers, New York, under the names "Lou Long" and "Lou Gerry." See Gallico, *Pride of the Yankees,* 61–62; and Bak, *American Classic,* 27.
12. Jack N. Arbolino, "The Lion Afield," in *A History of Columbia College on Morningside* (New York: Columbia University Press, 1954), 200.
13. Ibid., 214.
14. Paula S. Fass, *The Damned and the Beautiful: American Youth in the 1920s* (New York: Oxford University Press, 1977), 169–172, 186.
15. Arbolino, "Lion Afield," 216.
16. Bak, *American Classic,* 25.
17. Robert Pulleyn quoted in Robinson, *Iron Horse,* 52.
18. Ibid., 50.
19. Fass, *Damned and the Beautiful,* 7–8.
20. Fon W. Boardman, Jr., "After Class," in *History of Columbia,* 188.
21. *Columbia Spectator,* October 21, 1919.
22. Ibid., September 27, October 2, 1919.
23. Gallico, *Pride of the Yankees,* 63.
24. Fass, *Damned and the Beautiful,* 149–161.

25. Gallico, *Pride of the Yankees*, 64.

26. See Bak, *American Classic*, 29; and Ray Robinson, "Lou Gehrig: Columbia Legend and American Hero," *Columbia University Alumni Magazine*, Fall 2001, 3.

27. Fass, *Damned and the Beautiful*, 260–266. Fass argues that the 1920s were a turning point in terms of sexual conventions. Young college-going women were no longer willing to abide by the rigid practices of the Victorian era. While premarital intercourse was not the primary goal, petting and other forms of erotic experimentation were not only acceptable but also a perpetual concern on college campuses.

28. Arbolino, "Lion Afield," 201.

29. Jack Kavanagh, "Andy Coakley," in *The Ballplayers*, ed. Mike Shatzkin (New York: William Morrow, 1990), 200.

30. Arbolino, "Lion Afield," 214–215.

31. Robinson, *Iron Horse*, 53, 56.

32. Andy Coakley quoted in Graham, *A Quiet Hero*, 48.

33. "Gehrig Strikes Out Seventeen Batters, But Columbia Nine Loses to Williams, 5–1," *New York Tribune*, April 19, 1923.

34. George T. Moeschen quoted in Robinson, *Iron Horse*, 57.

35. Ibid., 57–58.

36. Donald Honig, *Power Hitters*, 27.

37. Bak, *American Classic*, 30. The homer proved to be the second longest hit in the history of South Field. On May 19, Lou smashed a more distant shot against Weslyan, one that cleared 116th Street and bounced off the steps of the library. See Robinson, *Iron Horse*, 59.

38. Hugh Fullerton, "Gehrig Biggest Star in College Baseball," *New York Tribune*, April 29, 1923.

39. William C. Kashatus, *Connie Mack's '29 Triumph: The Rise and Fall of the Philadelphia Athletics Dynasty* (Jefferson, NC: McFarland, 1999), 8, 36–44.

40. Graham, *Quiet Hero*, 55. Huntzinger later signed with the New York Giants but did not experience much success at the major league level. During a four-year career split between New York and the St. Louis Cardinals, he compiled a career record of 7–8 and a 3.60 ERA. See Wolff, *Baseball Encyclopedia*, 1929.

41. Interview with George Pollack (lawyer for Eleanor Gehrig estate), Atlantic Beach, NY, January 19, 2003.

42. Bak, *American Classic*, 31.

43. Lou Gehrig quoted in Harry T. Brundidge, "Lou Gehrig Gives Baseball Full Credit for Rescuing Parents and Self from New York Tenement District," *Sporting News*, December 25, 1930.

44. Stephen Holtje, "Lou Gehrig," in Shatzkin, *Ballplayers*, 381.

45. Andy Coakley quoted in " 'Hardest Hitter Ever,' Says Coakley of Young Gehrig," *New York World Telegram*, June 17, 1923.

Gehrig stands alongside manager Paddy O'Conner of the Hartford Senators, the Yankees' top farm club. *National Baseball Hall of Fame Library, Cooperstown, N.Y.*

# Krichell's "Can't Miss" Kid, 1923–1925

Paul Krichell never amounted to much as a major league baseball player. In his two seasons with the St. Louis Browns, he was a reserve catcher who batted just .222.[1] But when Krichell turned his attentions to scouting prospective talent, he had the intuition of a Hall-of-Famer. Lou Gehrig was his first big catch.

"I did not go out looking for Gehrig," he admitted, years after the signing. "I did not even know what position he played. But when he socked a couple of balls a mile, I sat up and took notice. I saw a tremendous youth with powerful arms and terrific legs. I said to myself, 'Krich, get busy. Here is a kid who can't miss.' "[2] Ed Barrow, the Yankee general manager who greatly admired Krichell's counsel and had hired him away from the Boston Red Sox just three years earlier, was skeptical over Krichell's prediction that he had discovered the "next Babe Ruth." Before Barrow would tender a contract, Gehrig had to prove himself by visiting Yankee Stadium and demonstrating his power-hitting ability.[3]

On that April day in 1923, Gehrig reported to the newly built stadium carrying his glove and spikes wrapped inside a newspaper.[4] Inside the clubhouse he was welcomed by the team's trainer, Doc Woods, who introduced the wide-eyed college star to Babe Ruth.

"Babe," said Woods, "I want you to meet Lou Gehrig from Columbia.

Ruth, seated in front of his locker tying his shoes, looked up, flashed a smile, and extended a meaty hand. "Hiya, kid," he said, offering his trademark greeting.[5] Shortly after, Yankee manager Miller Huggins escorted Gehrig onto the field and directed him to step into the batting cage to take a few cuts.

Since Lou didn't bring a bat, he chose one from a pile propped against the back of the cage. Unaware that the 48-ounce club he happened to choose belonged to Ruth himself, Gehrig took his place in the batter's box and smashed a half-dozen balls into the right-field bleachers.[6] The Babe was clearly mesmerized by the showcase. Not only did he ignore the fact that Lou was using one of his own bats—something the Babe considered inexcusable, as he cherished them—but he remarked to teammate Wally Pipp, "That kid sure can bust 'em!"[7] It was a rare compliment from the Sultan of Swat.

"We all knew that Lou was a big league ball player in the making," said Yankee pitcher Waite Hoyt, who watched Gehrig's slugging exhibition from the sidelines. "Nobody could miss on him. We didn't know what else he could do, or what position he would play. But it was a cinch that a young fellow who could hit like that couldn't be kept out of the major leagues."[8]

Barrow had seen enough. Convinced of Gehrig's talent, he signed him to a Yankee contract and ordered Huggins to give the young prospect a few at-bats before optioning him back to Hartford, where New York now operated its top farm club.

Gehrig's professional career began at the peak of the Yankee-Giant rivalry for the hearts of New York's fans. The National League Giants had been winning the competition until the 1920s, thanks to the efforts of manager John McGraw, who had molded his team into perennial contenders. The Yankees, on the other hand, suffered from a history of mediocrity.

Originally known as the "Highlanders," the team arrived in New York in 1903 when Ban Johnson, president of the American League, relocated the Baltimore franchise to the Empire City to cut into the Giants' extraordinary attendance figures. Frank Farrell, a former bartender who made a fortune through a politically sponsored gambling syndicate, and New York Police Chief "Big Bill" Devery purchased the club for $18,000 and attempted to establish a fan base in upper Manhattan. The new owners invested $200,000 to clear a rocky plot on the highest elevation of the borough and another $75,000 to build a wooden band-box ballpark there.[9] Located in Washington Heights between 165th and 168th Streets, "Hilltop Park" was quickly cobbled together with spruce and pine planks and, when completed, looked as miserable as the tenement slums in which the Yankees' fans lived. The grandstand sat 4,186, the bleachers down each line another 8,000, and the outfield seats yet another 2,500.[10] Fans were also permitted to stand on the field. Those who brought their own seats could pitch them in the outfield or even between the foul lines and the stands. Hilltop's outfield distances made the ballpark appear cavernous: 365 feet from home plate down the left-field line, 542 feet to center, and 400 feet down the right-field line.[11] But these were classic dimensions for the so-called "dead ball" era, when the game was played with a heavier baseball and strategies emphasized the hit-and-run, steal, and sacrifice bunt to score runs instead of the home run.

Managed by Clark Griffith, future owner of the Washington Senators, the Highlanders looked to capture their first pennant a year later, in 1904. The team was led by outfielder "Wee Willie" Keeler, who batted .343 with 185 hits and 22 stolen bases, and spitballer Jack Chesboro, who pitched three to four times a week and led the league with a remarkable 55 appearances, 454 innings pitched, and 41 victories.[12] Then, in a reflection of the haplessness that would haunt the club's future, the Highlanders blew the pennant on a wild pitch by Chesboro in the final game of the season. When asked by a sportswriter how he felt afterwards, Griffith responded with a more pointed question: "Can you imagine someone grabbing you by the throat, tearing your heart out by the roots and leaving you to die, suffering the tortures of the diamond?"[13]

During the next decade, the Highlanders spiraled into mediocrity, becoming perennial losers. Some hope arrived in 1915, however, when Colonel Jacob Ruppert and Tillinghast L'Hommedieu Huston purchased the club from Farrell and Devery for $460,000. By that time the team had changed its name to the Yankees and shared the Polo Grounds with the Giants.

Ruppert, a former Tammany-affiliated congressman from New York's Silk Stocking district, inherited his family's Manhattan brewery and enhanced his wealth through savvy real estate transactions. Aspiring to a higher social status, the German brewer, at age 22, ingratiated himself with the governor to gain entry into New York's Seventh Regiment, an exclusive unit composed of wealthy military buffs. Once he secured the honorary title "Colonel," Ruppert fancied himself a gentleman-bachelor and indulged in race cars, yachting, and women. He was also a frustrated pitcher who failed in a bid to make John McGraw's Giants, and therefore set his sights on owning a team.[14]

Huston, an engineer who led a volunteer regiment of builders during the Spanish-American War, made his wealth through government construction projects in Cuba. Returning to the United States, he built an extravagant baroque-styled mansion on a 30,000-acre estate in Georgia and proceeded to ingratiate himself into New York society. An overweight, affable man who preferred to be called "Til" by his intimates, Huston's business partnership with Ruppert was a marriage of convenience intended to gain him entry into New York's upper crust.[15] Both men loved to win, however, and were determined to build a championship dynasty that would rival, if not make New York's fans forget about, the Giants.

While Huston receded into the background, Ruppert made sweeping changes in Yankee personnel, both on the field and in the front office. After cleaning house, he hired "Wild Bill" Donovan as the team's new manager. Ruppert was banking on a repeat performance of Donovan's previous success with the Detroit Tigers, a team he piloted to three straight pennants between 1907 and 1909. Shortly after, Ruppert informed the other club owners that he was prepared to purchase any unwanted stars. With a failing economy and the Federal League luring away his players, Connie Mack of the Philadelphia Athletics was among the first takers. Mack gave away Bob Shawkey, an outstanding young hurler, for the bargain basement sum of $15,000.[16] Shawkey would become a consistent twenty-game winner for the Yankees. A year later, the A's manager sold Frank "Home Run" Baker, the game's best third baseman at the time, to New York for $25,000.[17]

When Donovan couldn't produce a pennant after three years, Ruppert fired him and brought in Miller Huggins, the scrappy little second baseman-turned-manager of the St. Louis Cardinals. Huggins, nicknamed the "Mighty Mite" because of his scrawny 5-foot, 6-inch stature, had prodded two third-place finishes out of an average team. In doing so, he captured the interest of American League president Ban Johnson, who urged Ruppert to hire him.[18] Under Huggins' leadership the Yankees steadily climbed from fourth place in 1918 to world champions in 1923. Just as critical to New York's success was the acquisition of George Herman Ruth and Ed Barrow from the Boston Red Sox.

Prior to 1920, Boston was the uncontested champion of the American League, having captured five pennants and five World Series since the establishment of the circuit in 1903. Babe Ruth had been the key to their success, both at the plate and on the pitcher's mound. In 1916 he posted a 23–12 record and a league-leading 1.75 ERA for the world champion Red Sox. He won a career-high twenty-four games the following season when he posted a .325 batting average in 123 at-bats. Ruth's twenty-nine consecutive scoreless innings in World Series play stood as a record for more than forty years, establishing him as one of the best hurlers in the history of the game. But Boston's manager Ed Barrow realized that his star hurler's bat was too powerful to remain idle on days he didn't pitch. Therefore, in 1918, Barrow started playing Ruth in the outfield and made him a regular in 1919, when he hit a major league-record 29 home runs.[19]

Despite his team's remarkable success, Red Sox owner Harry Frazee felt no special allegiance to them. In 1919, when he needed money to bankroll his Broadway musicals, Frazee sold Ruth to the Yankees for the record sum of $100,000.[20] Not only did the Babe revolutionize the game, shattering his own home-run record with the 54 he hit in 1920, but he changed the dynamics of New York's baseball market by attracting large crowds to Yankee games. Barrow, furious at having lost his franchise player, joined the Yankee front office the following year, and the balance of power shifted from Boston to New York.[21]

Barrow was a consummate wheeler-dealer who enjoyed an extensive network of connections in baseball. Having been a manager, general manager, and owner in the International League and a manager of two major league clubs, "Cousin Ed," as he was known in baseball circles, was a shrewd evaluator of talent. After being appointed Yankee general manager in 1921, Barrow proceeded to buy or trade for the star players he managed in Boston, giving up very little in return. Over the next few years, he robbed the Red Sox roster of such star performers as catcher Wally Schang, shortstop Everett Scott, and pitchers Waite Hoyt, "Bullet Joe" Bush, "Sad Sam" Jones, and Herb Pennock. He also established a strong farm system and hired George Weiss, a friend and former minor league business manager, to run it.

Barrow's hard-line approach and terrible temper discouraged players from challenging his contract offers. At the same time, he earned the trust and loyalty of Miller Huggins by persuading Ruppert and Huston to stay out of the clubhouse and by respecting his manager's right to handle the on-field matters as he pleased.[22] In 1923, when Ruppert bought out Huston for an estimated $1.25 million, Barrow purchased 10 percent of the team for $300,000, further strengthening his position in the organization.[23] Most important, Barrow created a winning atmosphere by providing Huggins with the players to clinch three straight pennants in 1921, 1922, and 1923. But it still wasn't enough to displace the Giants.

New York's National Leaguers defeated the Yankees in back-to-back "Subway Series" in 1921 and 1922. To add insult to injury, McGraw and Giants owner Charles Stoneham ejected the Yankees from the Polo Grounds after the 1922 season. Forced to find a new home, Ruppert and Huston purchased a ten-acre plot in the Bronx just across the Harlem River for $500,000.[24]

Completed in just 284 days by the White Construction Company of New York, the stadium cost $2,500,000 and was the most majestic ballpark constructed to that date.[25] Its double-decked grandstand plus a mezzanine accommodated more than 55,000 fans, and its dimensions were tailored to Ruth's power hitting. The right-field fence was 295 feet away from home plate, hardly a challenge for the Bambino's towering drives. Right-handed hitters, on the other hand, were frustrated by the long, deepening angle that began down the left-field line and extended into center, a formidable 490 feet away from home plate. Known as "Death Valley," the left- and center-field dimensions transformed many a long drive into a routine fly-ball.[26] If there was any doubt that Yankee Stadium was, as sportswriter Fred Lieb called it, "The House That Ruth Built," it was eliminated on opening day (April 18, 1923), when the Bambino christened the park with a three-run homer to defeat the Boston Red Sox 4–1.[27]

On June 16, Lou Gehrig made his major league debut against the St. Louis Browns, replacing Wally Pipp at first base. It was the ninth inning of a game that was out of reach for the hapless Brownies. Gehrig made one put-out but did not get the chance to hit.[28] Lou spent most of the next five weeks on the bench next to Huggins, occasionally getting into a game as a pinch hitter or late-inning substitute for Pipp. When his parents came to see him play and discovered that he was riding the bench, they were dumbfounded. "They pay you to be a bummer?" remarked Pop Gehrig. "You do nothing. What kind of a business is this?"[29] Any explanation Lou might have given would have been lost on them. The Gehrigs' naiveté would only diminish with more exposure to the game.

On July 19, Lou collected his first major league hit—a pinch-hit single—off the Browns' Elam Vangilder at Sportsman's Park in St. Louis. A few days later, he was sent to Hartford to get more playing experience.[30]

During his first two weeks in the Eastern League, Gehrig struggled, hitting just .062. Desperately afraid of failing and having used his signing bonus to pay for his parents' medical bills, Lou was depressed and broke. "When he was in that slump, I'd never seen anyone suffer so much," recalled Harry Hesse, Gehrig's roommate at Hartford. "He took everything to heart. He'd get so miserable that it was pretty tough to pull him out of it."[31] Some of the veteran minor leaguers, much less talented players who were more concerned with skirt-chasing and carousing than making it to the majors, took Gehrig out drinking.[32] Soon he began to tag along, hoping to make a few friends on the ball club. Concerned about the youngster's future, Hartford manager Paddy O'Conner wired Barrow, who sent Paul Krichell up to Connecticut to talk with Gehrig.

Krichell, who was scouting some players in Spartanburg, South Carolina, hopped a night train to Hartford and watched Lou struggle through another 0-for-4 performance. After the game, the Yankee scout gave him a pep talk. Gehrig admitted that he was afraid that he couldn't live up to the high praise he had been given in the Hartford newspapers, and that he was considering quitting baseball altogether. Realizing that his young prospect was haunted by a fear of failure, Krichell reminded Lou that the Yankees had a lot of confidence in his abilities and that "the most important thing a young ballplayer can learn is that he can't be good every day."[33]

O'Conner later echoed Krichell's message. "You have a wonderful career ahead of you," he told Gehrig, "but you have to accept the good with the bad. Nothing can stop you, except Lou Gehrig." Expressing his concern that Lou was surrounding himself by the wrong players on the team, O'Conner reminded

Lou that he can "wind up a rich man from the game" for just "six months of work, two hours of hustle each afternoon, for one-hundred and fifty-four games," but only if he removed himself from "that gang you're traveling with."[34] Gehrig took his manager's advice, and his fortunes soon changed. In the fifty-nine games he played for Hartford, Lou finished the season with a .304 average and collected 69 hits, including 24 home runs, 13 doubles, and 8 triples.[35]

By the time Hartford's season ended, the Yankees were already coasting to a third straight pennant, sixteen games ahead of second-place Detroit. Huggins promoted Lou in mid-September, after the Yankees had clinched the flag, to give him some major league experience without the pressure of a pennant race. However, some of the players did not appreciate Lou's insertion into the line-up. Bullet Joe Bush, a veteran pitcher who was determined to seal his second straight twenty-win season that year, complained about Huggins' decision. "Don't put that damn clown out there at first," he fumed. "This game may not mean anything to the team, but it means a lot to me. That guy will gum it up."

Never one to let his players order him around, Huggins ignored the complaint and started Gehrig at first against the Washington Senators. When Lou misplayed a bunt, allowing a run to score in the early innings of the game, Bush glared at the rookie and dressed him down in front of their teammates: "Ya stupid college punk! Where's your brains, dummy?" Gehrig, on the verge of tears, just stared at the ground. But in the eighth inning, with the Yankees trailing 5–2, he managed to redeem himself by hitting a bases-clearing double to tie the game, and he then scored the go-ahead run on a single to win the contest, 6–5. "Look kid," said Bush, greeting Lou in the dugout afterwards, "you may not be so hot with the glove, but you sure can pound the ball."[36]

On September 27, Gehrig played his last game of the 1923 season and collected his first major league home run against Bill Peary of the Red Sox at Boston's Fenway Park.[37] Although Wally Pipp, the team's regular first baseman, had injured his ankle and Huggins requested that Lou be activated for the World Series, the request had to be approved by baseball commissioner Judge Kenesaw Mountain Landis because Gehrig had joined the Yankees after the September 1 eligibility deadline. Landis agreed to give his consent if the arrangement was cleared by John McGraw, manager of the National League's pennant-winning Giants. McGraw, out of spite, refused, telling Landis, "If the Yankees have an injury, its their hard luck."[38] Therefore, Lou sat out the Series, Pipp played with an injured ankle, and the Yankees won their first world championship.

Gehrig left the Yankees with a good impression by the end of the 1923 campaign. In the thirteen games Lou played for New York, he hit .423, with

4 doubles, a triple, and a home run. The performance convinced Barrow that Gehrig had a bright future with the Yankees, and he later refused to trade him to Louisville of the American Association for centerfielder Earle Combs, a top prospect the Yankee general manager desired.[39]

Invited to the Yankees' spring training camp in New Orleans in 1924, Lou hoped to win a job as a regular. While he continued to impress the Yankee brass with his on-field performance, Gehrig had problems fitting in with a rowdy veteran squad that played hard but partied even harder. "When I broke into this league the Yankees, mostly oldsters, were clannish and sullen toward the rookies," he remembered. "They made it hard for us. You had to be one of the clan off the field, too. If you weren't, you didn't get a break. Sometimes, when I wanted to take batting practice, I found my favorite bat sawed in four parts, the kind of meanness that was hard to understand."[40]

Gehrig's poor financial circumstances didn't help either. Since players did not receive any salary payment until the season began, Lou would have to make the $14 he had last the entire month. Having no pocket money or friends, he spent most of his time alone. "I was glad the team worked out every day from eleven to one, so I could just skip lunch," he admitted years later.[41] After he spent his last few dollars, Gehrig went out looking for a part-time job waiting on tables. When Huggins learned of his prized rookie's circumstances, he gave him a $100 advance and told him to "stop looking for a job."[42] He also arranged for Lou to room with Benny Bengough, a 26-year-old catcher who had joined the Yankees the year before. They soon became good friends.

When the Yankees went north to begin the season, Gehrig was still unsure of his status. A few days before the opener Huggins told him of his intentions to send him back to the minors to gain more playing experience. But before Lou could become discouraged by the decision, the Yankee skipper added, "When I get you back in the fall, you'll be here to stay."[43] Before he returned to Hartford, Gehrig collected six hits in a dozen at-bats.

Confident now that he would make the majors, the young slugger rejoined Hartford and hit at a .383 clip, leading the team into a pennant race. With his 21st birthday near, Lou asked his manager if he could return to New York to celebrate with his parents. When O'Conner reminded him that the team was in the heat of a pennant race and that the game against second-place Worcester was scheduled for June 19, his birthday, Gehrig withdrew the request. But after his double, triple, and home run pacing Hartford to a 9–8 victory, O'Conner permitted his star to return home to celebrate a belated birthday.[44]

Lou finished the Eastern League season with a .369 average, collecting 186 hits, including 40 doubles, 13 triples, and 37 home runs.[45] Huggins immediately called him up before the September 1 deadline, making him eligible for post-season play. Used mostly as a pinch hitter, Gehrig hit .500 and experienced his first ejection from a major league game. It came on September 21 at Detroit. After hitting a 2-run single to put the Yankees ahead of the Tigers in the eighth inning of a close game, Lou was picked off first base. Ty Cobb, known for his vitriolic jockeying of opposing players, relished the opportunity to initiate the Yankee rookie. When the Tigers' player-manager took his place in the third base coaching box in the bottom of the inning, he launched a nasty verbal assault against Gehrig. Lou suffered some of the abuse, but finally charged across the infield. Before he could lay a hand on Cobb, he was tossed from the game. It was the first of just 5 ejections Lou experienced during his career, because he preferred to keep a level head and let his bat do the talking.[46]

There would be no World Series for the Yankees in 1924. Despite the brilliant pitching of Pennock (21–9) and Hoyt (18–13) and the prodigious hitting of Ruth (.378, 46 HR, 121 RBIs), Meusel (.325, 12 HR, 120 RBIs), and Pipp (.295, 9 HR, 113 RBIs), the Yanks finished second, two games behind the Washington Senators.[47]

During the off-season, trade rumors involving Gehrig circulated once again. One rumor had him going to the Red Sox for first baseman Phil Todt.[48] Another suggested that Lou would be packaged with veteran pitcher Bullet Joe Bush and sent to the St. Louis Browns for veteran spitballer Urban Shocker.[49] "That's the silliest thing ever written," exclaimed Huggins when informed of the trade talk. "If I trade Gehrig I should be shot at sunrise!"[50] In fact, Huggins was planning to overhaul his line-up in 1925 and Gehrig figured prominently in the scheme. His decision to make changes was reinforced by the poor start the Yankees experienced in the spring of 1925.

Ruth, the cornerstone of the organization, was struck down with stomach problems on the way north from spring training. The so-called "bellyache heard round the world" sidelined him until June and even then he wasn't able to find his stroke, hitting just .246.[51] Unable to make up for Ruth's offensive production, the Yanks fell to seventh place and aging veterans like first baseman Wally Pipp, catcher Wally Schang, centerfielder Whitey Witt, and shortstop Everett Scott came under Huggins' close scrutiny.

Pipp, a 32-year-old veteran, had played for the Yanks for ten years, helping them to three pennants with a cumulative batting average of .310 during his tenure.[52] During the Dead Ball era, he was a serious home-run threat, hitting twelve round trippers to lead the team in 1916 and capturing the club's crown again the following year with 9.[53] But by 1925 he knew he was nearing the end of his career. Like other veterans who were being challenged by younger prospects, Pipp might have resented Gehrig, realizing that he was being groomed to take his own job. Instead, he helped Lou with his fielding, teaching him the proper footwork around the bag, how to take throws from the various position players, and how to pick balls in the dirt.[54] Gehrig listened and learned. He also appreciated Pipp's effort, realizing how difficult it was to be accepted by the clannish veterans.

The Yankees opened the 1925 campaign with Gehrig on the bench and Pipp playing first. Lou appeared in just eleven games during the first two months of the season, but not once did he complain. Huggins had assured him that his time was soon approaching.[55] Then, on June 1, Gehrig was called on to pinch hit for "Pee Wee" Wanninger, the Yankee shortstop, in the eighth inning of a game against the Washington Senators. Lou stepped up to the plate to face Walter Johnson and lofted the second pitch into left field where Goose Goslin retired him.[56] It was an unremarkable event for those on hand to see it, but that plate appearance marked the beginning of Gehrig's 2,130-consecutive-game streak. Interestingly, Wanninger, the hitter Lou was called on to replace, had put an end to Everett Scott's 1,307-consecutive-game streak when he replaced the aging shortstop on May 5.[57] Now Gehrig would be challenging Scott's record.

The next day, June 2, Pipp was beaned in batting practice and knocked semi-conscious. He was rushed to the hospital where he spent the next two weeks recuperating.[58] Gehrig was inserted into the sixth slot in the line-up—behind Ruth, who hit clean-up, and Bob Meusel, who hit fifth—and went 3 for 5 with a double that day.[59] In the field, Lou had 8 put-outs and 1 assist.[60] While he continued to start at first base, Huggins used a pinch hitter for him on three occasions that same month.[61] Gehrig's status as the Yankees' regular first baseman might have been tenuous at best, but the sportswriters welcomed the change, along with the others Huggins had made to the line-up. On June 3, John Kieran of the *New York Tribune* wrote:

> Miller Huggins shot the works. Facing a drop into the cellar with a former championship team, he yanked out three of his regulars at the stadium yesterday, sent his youngsters out to play, and the revamped Yankees came through to victory over the world champion Senators. Aaron Ward, Wally Pipp and Wally Schang were benched in favor of Howard Shanks, Lou Gehrig and Benny Bengough. The youngsters romped about the greensward in joyous fashion and contributed more than their share of the 16 soaring safeties amassed by the Yankees. Gehrig got a single in the second, a double in the third, and a single in the fifth. Now then, boys, all together—Rah, Rah, Rah, Columbia![62]

Despite the fact that the Yankees finished the season in seventh place, 28½ games behind the pennant-winning Senators, there were some encouraging developments. New York's .974 fielding average was the best in the American League largely due to the rookie performances of catcher Benny Bengough (.993 fielding average), Gehrig (.989), and centerfielder Earle Combs (.979). Earle Combs, whose contract was purchased from Louisville of the American Association two years earlier, replaced Whitey Witt in centerfield, and Urban Shocker and Dutch Ruether were added to a formidable pitching staff that already featured veterans Herb Pennock, Waite Hoyt, and Bob Shawkey. In addition, Combs compiled an impressive .342 batting average in his first season as a regular, and Gehrig had also proven himself offensively, hitting .295 with 20 home runs and 68 RBIs in 126 games.[63]

"Only Lou's willingness and lack of conceit will make him into a complete ballplayer," said Huggins, when asked about Gehrig's future with the Yankees. "That and those muscles are all he has."[64] Maybe so, but those qualities were sufficient enough for the Yankees to trade their veteran first baseman Wally Pipp to Cincinnati, where he finished his career and later became the subject of the popular baseball trivia question: Who did Lou Gehrig replace at first base when he began his 2,130-consecutive-game streak in 1925?

## NOTES

1. Frank V. Phelps, "Paul Krichell," in *Ballplayers*, Shatzkin, 588.
2. Paul Krichell quoted in Honig, *Power Hitters*, 27.
3. Glenn Stout and Richard A. Johnson, *Yankees Century: 100 Years of New York Yankees Baseball* (Boston: Houghton Mifflin, 2002), 109.
4. Robinson, *Iron Horse*, 66.
5. Bak, *American Classic*, 35.
6. Robinson, *Iron Horse*, 68.
7. Ruth to Wally Pipp quoted in Babe Ruth with Bob Considine,*The Babe Ruth Story* (New York: Dutton, 1948; reprinted by Penguin, 1992), 125.
8. Waite Hoyt quoted in Graham, *Quiet Hero*, 70.
9. Stout and Johnson, *Yankees Century*, 3–14.
10. Ibid., 16; and Dave Anderson et al., *The New York Yankees Illustrated History* (New York: St. Martin's Press, 2002), 6.
11. Ritter, *Lost Ballparks*, 93.
12. Stout and Johnson, *Yankees Century*, 30–31, 36.
13. Griffith quoted in ibid., 39.
14. Gallagher and LaConte, *Yankee Encyclopedia*, 331–332.
15. Ibid., 330; and Stout and Johnson, *Yankees Century*, 66.

16. Stout and Johnson, *Yankees Century*, 68.

17. Ibid., 71.

18. A. D. Suehsdorf, "Miller Huggins," in *Ballplayers*, Shatzkin, 499–500.

19. Tom Gallagher and Christopher D. Renino, "Babe Ruth," in *Ballplayers*, Shatzkin, 949.

20. Anderson, *Yankees Illustrated History*, 14.

21. Gallagher and LaConte, *Yankee Encyclopedia*, 335.

22. Ibid., 334–336.

23. Anderson, *Yankees Illustrated History*, 26. Ruppert and Huston were never comfortable with each other. When Ruppert hired Miller Huggins in 1917 without Huston's consent, the action further estranged the partners. The breaking point came when Huston, who was instrumental in purchasing Ruth from the Red Sox, introduced the star slugger to New York's nightlife, tempting him to violate the team curfew.

24. Stout and Johnson, *Yankees Century*, 96.

25. Anderson, *Yankees Illustrated History*, 21–23.

26. Ibid., 21.

27. Ibid., 25–26.

28. Graham, *Quiet Hero*, 72.

29. Heinrich Ludwig Gehrig quoted in Robinson, *Iron Horse*, 71.

30. Bak, *American Classic*, 36.

31. Harry Hesse quoted in ibid., 36.

32. Gallico, *Pride of the Yankees*, 52–55.

33. Paul Krichell quoted in Graham, *Quiet Hero*, 84.

34. Paddy O'Conner quoted in Robinson, *Iron Horse*, 72.

35. Bak, *American Classic*, 39.

36. Bush quoted in ibid., 40–41.

37. Robinson, *Iron Horse*, 76.

38. John McGraw quoted in ibid, 76. Gehrig believed that McGraw refused to approve his eligibility for the 1923 World Series to spite him for having left Hartford two years earlier when he returned to Columbia University. See Charles C. Alexander, *John McGraw* (New York: Penguin, 1989), 335, note 22.

39. Honig, *Power Hitters*, 27.

40. Gehrig quoted in Robinson, *Iron Horse*, 81.

41. Ibid., 80.

42. Miller Huggins quoted in Robinson, *Iron Horse*, 82.

43. Ibid.

44. Bak, *American Classic*, 45.

45. Honig, *Power Hitters*, 27.

46. Bak, *American Classic*, 46.

47. Gallagher and LaConte, *Yankee Encyclopedia*, 377.

48. "Lou Gehrig," The Baseball Page Web site, 2001, www.baseballlibrary.com/base

balllibrary/ballplayers/G/Gehrig_Lou.stm (2002). Fortunately for the Yankees, the Red Sox rejected the Todt deal. Todt never hit higher than .278 in six years as the Red Sox regular first baseman.

49. Robinson, *Iron Horse*, 84. The trade rumor involving Urban Shocker was floated by Bozeman Bulger of the *New York Evening World* in December 1924. Bulger contended that the Browns needed a young first baseman to replace the aging George Sisler. Shocker was eventually traded to the Yankees in exchange for Bush and two other lesser known players.

50. Huggins quoted in ibid., 85.

51. Graham, *Quiet Hero*, 98–99. New York sportswriter W. O. McGeehan called Ruth's ailment the "bellyache heard round the world" because of all the press coverage it captured. One of Ruth's biographers, Marshall Smelser, argues that the bellyache was really syphilis, brought on by a little too much carousing. See Marshall Smelser, *The Life That Ruth Built: A Biography* (New York: Quadrangle, 1975), 315.

52. Honig, *Power Hitters*, 29.

53. Ernie Harwell, "Wally Pipp's Big League Career Forgotten with a 'Headache,' " *Baseball Digest*, September 2000, 58.

54. Graham, *Quiet Hero*, 93. Paul Gallico credits Yankee coach Charlie O'Leary with helping Gehrig to learn first base. See Gallico, *Pride of the Yankees*, 89–90.

55. Honig, *Power Hitters*, 29.

56. Bak, *American Classic*, 47.

57. Ibid., 40.

58. Robinson, *Iron Horse*, 87. Years later, Pipp denied being hit in batting practice on the day that Gehrig took over for him at first base. "I was beaned all right," he said. "But it was a month after Lou took my place." See Harwell, "Wally Pipp's Big League Career Forgotten with a 'Headache.' "

59. Robinson, *Iron Horse*, 88

60. Graham, *Quiet Hero*, 103.

61. Holtje, "Lou Gehrig"; and Bak, *American Classic*, 152.

62. John Kieran, "Huggins Sends in Youngsters to Beat Washington," *New York Herald Tribune*, June 3, 1925.

63. Wolff, *Baseball Encyclopedia*, 243.

64. Huggins quoted in Bak, *American Classic*, 86.

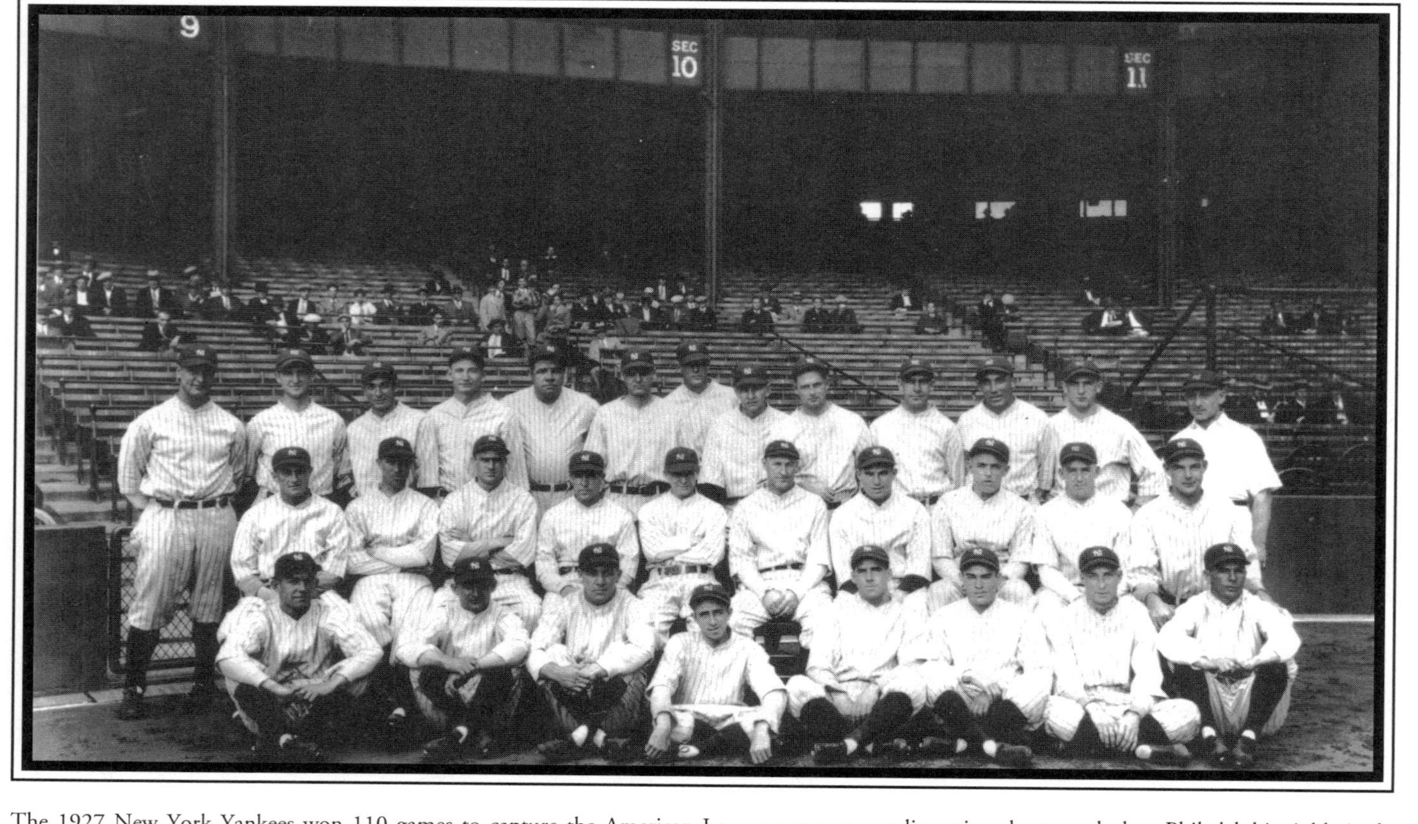


The 1927 New York Yankees won 110 games to capture the American League pennant, outdistancing the second-place Philadelphia Athletics by nineteen games. Led by the powerful hitting tandem of Ruth and Gehrig, the team swept the Pittsburgh Pirates in the World Series in four games. The 1927 Yankees are still widely regarded as the greatest team ever in the history of baseball. *National Baseball Hall of Fame Library, Cooperstown, N.Y.*

4

# Yankee Dynasty, 1926–1928

The 1920s were an era of excitement, restlessness, and change for New York City. World War I had just ended. Business was booming. Radio, movies, tabloid journalism, and the recording industry radically altered the rhythms of everyday life. Almost overnight, the automobile became an institution, freeing people to travel where they pleased. Subways, trolleys, and ferry boats connected the five boroughs, joining the urban landscape with its rural surroundings. Pleasant suburbs began to flourish where a few years before there had been miles of farmland. Happiness, success, and enjoyment—the "good life"—were increasingly defined by what a person owned or the freedom he or she enjoyed. New manners and new morals made it a good time to be alive, especially for the young. Old rules were changing. Women were shortening their hair and their skirts. The tin lizzy was quickly becoming a four-wheeled sofa for youth determined to listen only to their libidos. Bootleg booze, flappers, and pinstripes were the new rules. The dance was the Charleston, the music jazz.

The Roaring Twenties also brought a new popularity to baseball. The ball was livelier than ever before. Prior to 1920, baseball was a low-scoring game. It emphasized the hit-and-run, stolen base, squeeze play, and bunt. The ball remained largely inside the park and teams focused on manufacturing runs, inning by inning. But in 1920 the "inside game" yielded to the lively ball. Home runs were flying out of ballparks at a record pace, especially in the American League, thanks to Babe Ruth.[1] In New York, baseball fans divided their loyalties between the Yankees and their National League rivals, John McGraw's Giants and the Brooklyn Dodgers. But Colonel Jacob Ruppert, who liked to win pennants early and often, was determined to capture the affections of the fans for his Yankees. Not only did he build the grandest stadium in the history of the game to accommodate the large crowds he anticipated, but he invested the fortunes of his brewing empire in player salaries to lure a crop of colorful—as well as highly talented—personalities. With names like Tony "Poosh 'Em Up" Lazzeri, "Jumpin' Joe" Dugan, and the "Sultan of Swat" himself, Babe Ruth, the Bronx Bombers had little difficulty capturing the imagination of fans, young and old alike. The city's ballplayers became as popular as movie stars, in part because of the expanded coverage they were given by the radio as well as by the sportswriters.[2] The most talented scribes—Heywood Broun, Damon Runyan, and Grantland Rice—were instrumental in promoting public hero worship of players who were sharp-witted and strong, reckless and carefree, brutally candid and shamelessly self-indulgent—much like the Roaring Twenties itself.[3]

If the Yankee lifestyle revolved around "drinking, wenching, and clouting the ball," as sportswriter Paul Gallico once remarked, then Lou Gehrig was woefully out of place, being good for just one of those three activities.[4] In fact, Gehrig once admitted to the sportswriters that he had "everything he wanted at home" in suburban New Rochelle, where he lived with his parents.[5] Still shy and quiet, Lou led an unremarkable life off the playing field and continued to defer to his mother, even though he was now the primary income earner.[6] But on the playing field, Gehrig was on the fringe of superstardom. His ascendancy into the ranks of baseball immortality occurred between 1926 and 1928 when the Yankees won three pennants and two world championships. This so-called "dynasty"—and particularly the 1927 team—is widely considered to be the greatest collection of players ever in the history of baseball.[7] While the reputation is debatable, Gehrig's value to the club is not.

The 1926 campaign proved to be a remarkable comeback after the Yanks' seventh-place finish the previous year. Huggins had made a number of vital changes to his line-up. In addition to replacing first baseman Wally Pipp with Gehrig, the "Mighty Mite" had a new keystone combination in shortstop Mark Koenig and second baseman Tony Lazzeri.

After defeating the Red Sox 12–11 on opening day at Boston's Fenway Park, the Yankees stayed hot until early September, when the Cleveland Indians took four straight from the New York.[8] The Yanks' first-place lead was narrowed to just three games, creating a three-way race for the pennant between the Yankees, Indians, and Philadelphia A's. Gehrig batted fifth in the line-up and proved to be the club's deadliest hitter in the clutch. Intensely competitive, he often blamed himself for the team's losses, or, on those rare occasions, when he failed to deliver at the plate. In the eighth inning of a mid-September game against the Chicago White Sox, for example, the Yankees were down by a run with two men on base and Lou at the plate. A hit would have tied the game and a long single would have put the team ahead. Lou swung at the first pitch and popped the ball up for an easy infield out. The Yankees still managed to rally and win the game. It didn't matter. Amidst the post-game celebration, Lou was seen sitting on the bench in the corner of the dugout sobbing, feeling guilty that he had failed his team when they needed him most.

"Other guys would take refuge in gobs of cynical, muddied profanity," observed teammate Waite Hoyt. "But not Lou. He took everything on a ball field so seriously."[9] Huggins, who also witnessed the scene, was enamored of his young first baseman. The Yankee skipper found Gehrig's innocence to be a refreshing asset on a team of hard-living veterans. He realized that Lou's tears were motivated by a combination of high expectations and the kind of insatiable competitiveness he wanted in all his players. "Lou has become a positive influence to the entire team," Huggins told the sportswriters near the end of the 1926 campaign. "You get a player with that kind of spirit and it spreads like a contagion to the others. He has come along much faster than I dared to expect."[10]

In mid-September, the Yankees, with a four-game lead, traveled to Cleveland for a six-game series with the Indians. Cleveland won the opening double-header, but the Yanks rebounded to win the remaining four games. Gehrig starred in the Yankees' 8–3 victory on September 19, hitting 3 doubles, a home run, and knocking in 5 runs. A week later, the Yankees clinched the pennant, sweeping a double-header from the St. Louis Browns, 10–2 and 10–4.[11]

New York faced the St. Louis Cardinals in the World Series. Only Rogers Hornsby, St. Louis' fiery manager, seemed to believe that his club had any chance against the powerful Yankees. His secret weapon was 39-year-old Grover Alexander, a seasoned right-hander and future Hall-of-Famer who once starred for the Philadelphia Phillies. The Cards acquired Alexander from the Chicago Cubs for the waiver price of $4,000. It turned out to be the best bargain in the history of St. Louis baseball. The Series opened in the Bronx on October 2 before a crowd of 61,658. Gehrig won the game in the sixth when he singled home Ruth to give the Yanks a 2–1 lead. Those two runs were all Herb Pennock needed to close down the Cardinals on three hits for the opening victory. In Game 2, the Cards sent Alexander to the mound. After a shaky start in which he surrendered two runs, the St. Louis hurler set down twenty-one Yankee hitters in a row to win the game 6–2. The Series then shifted to St. Louis, where the Cardinals won Game 3 behind the masterful pitching of Jesse Haines, who limited the Yankees to just 5 hits and slugged a 2-run homer in the 5–0 whitewashing. The Yankees got revenge in Game 4 as Gehrig collected 2 hits, including a bases-clearing double, and Ruth hit 3 home runs to lead New York to a 10–5 romp. The Yankees won again the following day in ten innings, 3–2, and the Series returned to New York. Alexander took the mound again for the Cards in Game 6 and won 10–2, tying the Series at three games apiece and setting the stage for the seventh and deciding contest.[12] Again, Alexander was the hero.

With two outs in the bottom of the seventh and the bases loaded with Yankees, Alexander came on in relief of Haines to strike out the dangerous Tony Lazzeri and to end the New York threat and preserve St. Louis's 3–2 lead. Alexander retired the Yankees in order in the eighth and allowed only Ruth to reach base in the ninth. With two outs and the Cards clinging to a one-run lead, the Bambino made the inexplicable mistake of attempting to steal second. St. Louis catcher Bob O'Farrell nailed him with a perfect throw, ending the Series and clinching the championship for St. Louis.[13]

Regardless of their performance in the Fall Classic, the 1926 Yankees were an impressive team. Pennock (23–11, 3.62 ERA), Urban Shocker (19–11), and Waite Hoyt (16–12) provided a formidable starting rotation. Rookies Tony Lazzeri (.275, 18 HR, 114 RBIs) and Mark Koenig (.271, 5 HR, 62 RBIs) gave the team a strong defensive middle infield, while Gehrig (.313, 16 HR, 107 RBIs) and Dugan (.288, 1 HR, 64 RBIs) provided some offensive fire power at the corners. The outfield was even more productive. Ruth had another monster year (.372, 47 HR, 145 RBIs) and Combs (.299) and Meusel (.315, 81 RBIs) rounded out the offensive attack that came to be known as "Murderer's Row." Not surprisingly, the 1926 Yankees led the American League in five major offensive categories: runs (847), home runs (121), runs batted in (794), walks (642), and slugging percentage (.437). Their remarkable power hitting inspired Combs to coin the phrase "Five O'Clock Lightning," a reference to the nearby factory whistle that could be heard at Yankee Stadium when the team was on a late-inning rampage.[14] What's more, the statistics indicated that the Yankees had a very bright future ahead of them, one that could easily result in a championship dynasty.

Although Gehrig figured prominently in the Yankees' fortunes, he began to hear reports during the off-season that Huggins was looking for a right-handed hitting veteran first baseman and it angered him.[15] He realized that his manager was upset by his inability to take full advantage of his natural tendency to hit to right field, something that would have allowed him to hit more than the 16 homers he collected during the previous season. Lou also understood that he had more to learn about playing first base, especially going to his left, and also defending against a bunt. Huggins constantly reminded him of these shortcomings.[16] Although it is doubtful that the Yankee manager would have seriously considered trading Lou at this early stage of his career, the rumors about a right-handed hitting first baseman may have been created to spur Gehrig's progress in these two areas. As usual, Lou's response was to work harder. He left New Rochelle for spring training in St. Petersburg a week early, determined to improve his performance. "I don't know what all this talk of a right-handed hitting first baseman is about," he told the sportswriters shortly after he arrived. "If this guy is being considered because he may be more effective in hitting left-handed pitching, I can hit left-handers just as well as right-handers, and just as far."[17]

Lou put to rest any notion of being replaced in the Yankee line-up in spring training. "Gehrig looks bigger and better at the plate than he did last year," reported the *New York Telegraph*. He has been hitting solid smashes every time he walks to the plate. There isn't a harder working athlete on the squad."[18] Impressed by Gehrig's performance, Huggins decided to change the meat of his batting order. In 1926, Ruth hit third, Meusel fourth, and Gehrig fifth. But now the Yankee manager decided that Ruth, who was 32 years old and beginning to show signs of slippage, would be more effective at the plate if he had Gehrig hitting directly behind him in the order. Opposing pitchers would have to throw strikes to Ruth, rather than pitching around him, because Gehrig was even more dangerous with runners in scoring position. So Huggins switched Lou to the clean-up spot, with Meusel dropping down to fifth. It was a significant change because it allowed the Babe to become a greater home-run threat than he was in his prime. The switch also increased Gehrig's RBI production significantly since Ruth, hitting ahead of him, reached base nearly 50 percent of the time.[19] The offensive production of this switch was so great that the New York sports writers dubbed the Yankees, the "Bronx Bombers."

Most of the prognosticators picked the Philadelphia Athletics to capture the pennant in 1927. Connie Mack had assembled a nice mix of veterans like Ty Cobb, Eddie Collins, and Zack Wheat, who brought post-season experience and an encyclopedic knowledge of the game with them. They would also mentor such prospects as Mickey Cochrane, Jimmie Foxx, Al Simmons, and Lefty Grove, all of whom were on the verge of stardom. The oddsmakers made the A's a 9 to 5 favorite to win the flag, while New York, with an aging pitching staff, was at 3 to 1.[20] But New York would defy the bookies in 1927.

The Yanks opened the season on April 12 with an 8–3 victory over the A's and took the next two out of three against Philadelphia. At the end of April, the Bronx Bombers were 9–6 and tied for first place with the A's. They pulled away from the Mackmen in early May when they traveled to Philadelphia and swept the A's in a five-game series. From that point, the Yankees held sole possession of first place for the remainder of the season, and the attention of the New York fans turned to the home-run derby between Ruth and Gehrig.[21]

Ruth led Gehrig in the early going, but on May 7 Lou hit a grand slam against the White Sox to give the Yanks a 8–0 win and pulled ahead in the homer contest, 7–6. The Yankee first baseman also contributed two additional RBIs with a run-scoring double and a sacrifice to deep left field, proving that Huggins' switch in the line-up was going as planned. "If Mr. Ruth is going to show the way this season, he is not going to have the spotlight all to himself," wrote Bill Slocum of the *New York American*, noting that Gehrig's star was rising.[22] Ruth welcomed the challenge, going on a home-run binge in late May. By mid-June the Bambino enjoyed a six-homer lead over Lou, 24–18. Then, on June 23 at Boston's Fenway Park, Gehrig hit three home runs to pace the Yanks to an 11–4 victory over the Red Sox. It marked the first three-homer game of Lou's career and the first time *any* player had accomplished the feat at Fenway.[23] On July 4, Gehrig hit 2 home runs to pull ahead of Ruth, 28–27, as the Yanks swept a double-header against Washington, 12–1 and 21–1.[24] In mid-August, both sluggers were tied at 38 homers apiece and the Yankees enjoyed a thirteen-game lead over second-place Washington.[25] Shortly after, Ruth went on a tear, hitting 22 home runs to Gehrig's 9. By the time New York clinched the pennant on September 13, Ruth had 50 home runs to Gehrig's 45.[26] Lou would not hit another homer until September 28 and completed the regular season with a total of 47. Ruth won the derby, hitting his 60th on September 30 in the next to last day of the season to give the Bronx Bombers a 4–2 win over the Washington Senators at Yankee Stadium. Afterwards in the clubhouse, he bragged, "Sixty, count 'em, sixty! Let's see some other son of a bitch match that!"[27] But later, when asked if he thought anyone would ever break the record, the Bambino pointed in the direction of Gehrig's locker and said, "Wait till that bozo over there starts hitting again and they may forget that a guy named Ruth ever lived."[28]

Gehrig's home-run production tailed off in September because he was desperately worried about his mother, who had become seriously ill. After each home game, he'd rush off to the hospital and remain there until visiting hours ended. "I'm so worried about Mom that I can't see straight," he confided to sportswriter Frederick Lieb. "If I lost her I don't know what I would do."[29] In fact, Gehrig became so concerned that he considered sitting out the World Series just to be at her bedside. But when his mother's condition improved he decided to play.[30]

It staggers the imagination to consider what Gehrig's final statistics might have been in 1927 had his offensive production gone uninterrupted. He led the American League in three categories: runs batted in (175), doubles (52), and total bases (447). He finished second only to Ruth in home runs (47), runs scored (149), walks (109), and slugging percentage (.765). Together with his .333 batting average, those numbers earned him the league's most valuable player award.[31] More impressive are Ruth and Gehrig's cumulative totals: 107 home runs, 339 RBIs, and 307 runs scored. Together, Ruth and Gehrig accounted for 25 percent of all the home runs hit in the American League in 1927 and formed the most potent power-hitting duo in the history of the game.[32]

The Yankees faced the Pittsburgh Pirates in the shortest World Series on record lasting all of 74 hours and 15 minutes from the first pitch to the last. New York's four-game sweep resulted in the popular belief among writers and fans that Pittsburgh was hardly competitive, and that the team was intimidated by the way the Yankees crushed the ball in batting practice, before the start of Game 1.[33] In fact, Lloyd Waner, one of the Pirate stars, insisted that he never saw the Yanks take batting practice and though some of his teammates did, he "never heard any of them talk about what they saw."[34]

Nor were the Pirates pushovers. Pittsburgh had a well-balanced attack with several outstanding hitters, including Paul Waner (.380, 131 RBIs), his kid brother Lloyd (.355), third baseman Pie Traynor (.342, 106 RBIs), and George Grantham, Clyde Barnhart, and Kiki Cuyler, all of whom also hit over .300. The pitching was also formidable. Carmen Hill posted twenty-two wins, Lee Meadows had nineteen, Ray Kremer was 19–8 with a league-leading 2.47 ERA, and Vic Aldrige contributed another fifteen victories.[35] With that kind of hitting and pitching, only Game 3, an 8–1 Yankee victory, was out of reach for the Pirates. Game 2 was close until the bottom of the seventh inning, when the Yanks rallied to win 6–2. Games 1 and 4 went down to the final innings and were decided by one-run margins. In Game 1, Gehrig tripled in the Yankees' first run in his first at-bat. In the bottom of the first, the Pirates rallied to tie the game at 1–1, when Lloyd Waner singled, his brother Paul advanced him to third on a double, and Glenn Wright brought him home with a sacrifice fly to deep center field. The Yanks scored four more runs in the game, but had to hold on for the 5–4 victory as the Pirates knocked their ace Waite Hoyt out of the box in the eighth inning. Game 4 also came down to the final inning. With the score tied at 3–3 and the bases loaded with Yankees, Gehrig stepped to the plate to face Pittsburgh's John Miljus. Earle Combs tried to agitate Miljus by edging off third base with each pitch, but the hard-throwing right-hander was unfazed by the ploy as he struck out Gehrig and then fanned Meusel on three straight fastballs. Lazzeri was the next hitter and Miljus, bolstered by his success with the previous two hitters, put something extra on his fastball. The pitch broke so sharply that it eluded catcher Johnny Gooch, and Combs dashed home with the winning run to clinch the championship.[36]

With a record of 110–44, a winning percentage of .714, and a team batting average of .307, the 1927 Yankees were, statistically, one of the greatest teams in baseball history. The club scored more than 6 runs per game and held the opposition to fewer than 4 runs per game. Their penchant for clustering extra-base hits in the late innings not only warranted the nickname "Five O'Clock Lightning," but also made the line-up the most intimidating for any pitcher to face. Although it hardly seemed possible, the team's offensive production improved markedly from 1926. Gehrig's average jumped from .313 to .373, his home-run production from 16 to 47, and his RBI total from 107 to 175. Although Ruth's batting average dropped from .372 to .356, his home-run production jumped from 47 to 60, and his RBI total from 145 to 164. Other Yankees also enjoyed significant improvement. Combs' average increased from .294 to .356, Meusel's from .315 to .337, and Lazzeri's from .275 to .309. Even the light-hitting Koenig managed to improve his average from .271 to .285.[37]

The pitching staff was just as impressive. Waite Hoyt, the ace, went 22–7 with a 2.64 ERA. Herb Pennock (19–8, 3.00 ERA) was a solid number-two starter who relied on an effective change-up and a remarkable curve ball. Spitballer Urban Shocker (18–6, 2.84 ERA), Dutch Reuther (13–6, 3.38 ERA), and flame thrower George Pipgras (10–3, 4.11 ERA) rounded out the starting rotation. Wilcy Moore, a 30-year-old Oklahoma farmer whom the Yankees discovered pitching in the Piedmont League, posted a 13–3 record in relief, and an overall mark of 19–9.[38]

With superb pitching, a tight defense, and extraordinary hitting, the Yankees dominated the American League from the start of the season to its finish. Although their reputation as "Murderer's Row" gives them the perception of a one-dimensional team whose hitting was their dominant characteristic, they were, in fact, very well balanced. If excellence in a single season is the criteria for ranking the best team of all time, the 1927 Yankees would have a rightful claim to that title.[39] The 1927 Yankees have enjoyed that singular honor largely due to the fact that they played in New York, a media-rich haven where sports-writers have always blurred the distinction between myth and reality. They began shortly after the Yanks crushed the Pirates in the World Series, when James Harrison of the *New York Times* dubbed the team "the greatest in more than fifty years of baseball history." Not to be outdone, H. I. Phillips of the *New York Sun* called them a "team out of folklore and mythology."[40] The mythology has been fueled for more than three-quarters of a century now by some of baseball's most celebrated writers, including Ring Lardner, Grantland

Rice, Arthur Mann, Damon Runyon, and Paul Gallico. That many of these writers hailed from New York is not coincidental and, to be sure, the exploits of Babe Ruth—both on and off the playing field—only served to enhance the club's mythological reputation.

Ruth, keenly aware of his popularity, hired a publicist, Christy Walsh, to help him reap the financial rewards of it. After the 1927 World Series, Ruth, at the urging of Walsh, invited Gehrig to accompany him on a barnstorming tour arranged by the promoter. The tour began on October 12 in Trenton, New Jersey, where the two Yankees divided local players into two teams and played against each other. Ruth captained the "Bustin' Babes," and Gehrig captained the "Larrupin' Lous." During the next month, the two sluggers covered 8,000 miles, playing a total of twenty-one games in nine states from Rhode Island to California. More than 220,000 fans came out to see them at a time when many Americans who lived in the far West hadn't ever seen a major league ball game. Wherever Ruth and Gehrig performed there were overflow crowds that refused to be contained by makeshift police barriers surrounding the playing field. Youngsters often broke the line to shake hands with the Babe or get an autograph. Always the showman, Ruth encouraged them as it broke the monotony of the games, which were often quite dull. Lou often stood by watching the pandemonium in awe. Only when the Bambino insisted did he engage in the banter with his hero-worshipping fans.[41] When the tour ended on November 8, Walsh handed Gehrig a check for $10,000, a sum that amounted to $2,000 more than what the Yankees paid him for the entire season. Of course, Ruth earned much more from the tour, although it did not exceed the $70,000 the Yankees paid him for the 1927 campaign.[42]

In 1928 the Yankees won their third straight pennant, but it wasn't without difficulty. After winning thirty-four of the first forty-two games, the team held a comfortable twelve-game lead over the second-place Athletics. Then injuries began to take their toll. Lazzeri missed nearly forty games at second with a shoulder injury. Koenig was out for thirty games at shortstop. Dugan, hampered by a bad knee, missed sixty games at third. Meusel and Combs were also out of the line-up for extended periods. With the exceptions of Pipgras (24–13, 139 K, 3.38 ERA) and Hoyt (23–7, 3.36 ERA), the pitching declined. Pennock hurt his arm and missed the World Series. Moore's record dropped to 4–4. Ruether retired. Shocker, who became seriously ill in the spring, missed the entire season and died in September at age of 38. By September 8, the A's nudged the Yankees out of first place by one-half game.[43]

On Labor Day weekend, the Yanks rebounded, winning three of four games from the A's at Yankee Stadium. The Bronx Bombers regained first place on Sunday when they swept the Mackmen in a double-header, 5–0 and 7–3, before a sellout crowd of 85,264. The following day they defeated Philadelphia's ace, Lefty Grove, 5–3 to put the A's out of contention.[44] The Yanks went on to sweep the St. Louis Cardinals in four straight in the World Series. None of the games were close, with New York winning by three or more runs thanks to the impressive hitting of Ruth and Gehrig. Lou hit .545 with 4 home runs and 9 RBIs, while Ruth collected 10 hits in 16 at-bats for an extraordinary .625 average, the highest ever in World Series competition.[45] On the train ride back to New York, Ruth played master of ceremonies to the joyful pandemonium. Crowds met the train at every stop and the Babe greeted them all. Inside the passenger cars, he led the march to smash every straw boater in sight. By midnight Ruth was seizing every teammate or sportswriter and ripping the shirt off his back. Even the usually placid Gehrig joined in the raucous behavior.

"Lou and myself were at the head of the parade to get [Yankee owner] Jake Ruppert," recalled Ruth, years later. "He had locked himself in his drawing room with another old geezer whom we used to call 'Colonel Wattenberg.' We knocked at their door and Jake called out, 'Go away, Root!' But I told him this was no night for sleeping. I gave Lou a signal and we put our shoulders to the door and pushed right through the panel. I reached through, unlocked the door, and a moment later, Lou, myself and several others tumbled into the room. I got away with Jake's lavender pajama coat and Gehrig undressed Wattenberg, carrying off the top of his pajamas for a souvenir."[46]

The Yankees' three straight pennants and two consecutive world championships did not quiet the rumors of a blockbuster trade during the off-season. The city's sportswriters predicted that New York wasn't big enough for two superstars like Ruth and Gehrig. Since the Babe's popularity was too great, they reasoned, the Yanks would never part with the Bambino. But they could probably put Gehrig on the market for $50,000, or perhaps as much as $100,000.[47] In fact, Ruppert had no intention of breaking up his dynasty. Instead, he tried to increase his team's popularity throughout the American League by ordering new uniforms bearing numbers that coincided with the individual's place in the batting order. Ruth, for example, hit third and wore number 3. Gehrig hit in the clean-up spot and wore number 4. Not only did the new jerseys make the Yankees easily recognizable to fans in other ballparks, but they also set a new trend as other major league teams adopted the practice. To discourage the sportswriters' concern about the effect of Ruth's excessive weight on his playing ability, Ruppert also added dark blue pinstripes to the Yankees' plain, white home uniforms to make him appear trimmer.[48]

But these superficial changes could not hide the inevitable end of New York's dynasty. Even Huggins admitted as much when he predicted that "time and the law of averages will take care of it." When asked by the sportswriters in

May 1929 if he thought his Yanks would catch the Athletics who were off to a tremendous start, Huggins said "no," and identified "complacency" as the reason:

> I don't think these Yanks are going to win any more pennants, or at least, not this one. They're getting older and they're becoming glutted with success. They've been in three World Series in a row, remember, and they've won the last two Series in four straight. They've been getting fairly high salaries and they've taken a lot more out of baseball, a whole lot of money. They have stock market investments and these investments are giving them excellent returns at the moment. When they pick up a newspaper now, they turn to the financial page first and the sports page later. Those things aren't good for a club, not a club that is trying to beat a club like the one Mr. Mack has.[49]

Huggin's prediction proved accurate. On August 2, the A's enjoyed an 11½-game lead over the second-place Yankees. The "Mighty Mite" walked into Ruppert's office and said, "We'd better start getting ready for next year, Colonel."[50] With six weeks left in the season, the Yankee owner refused to believe that his team couldn't pull out another pennant. But the Yankees were mired in too many batting slumps. Gehrig himself was hitting just .300, 74 points lower than his final average of the previous season.[51]

On September 20, Huggins entered St. Vincent's Hospital in New York. He had been in poor health for weeks, but he continued to overexert himself in a desperate attempt to keep the Yankees from losing the championship. Five days later, as his team was playing the Boston Red Sox at Fenway Park, the fiery little manager died of blood poisoning. He was only 49 years old. When the fifth inning ended, both teams met at home plate and observed a moment of silence as the flag was lowered to half-mast.[52] A few days later, the Yankees gathered at his funeral to say good-bye. "We were a hard-boiled bunch, at least on the ballfield," recalled Babe Ruth, who had fought with Huggins during his early years in New York. "Tony Lazzeri, Waite Hoyt, Earle Combs, and myself—all of us—cursed Hug when he tried to harness our energies. We scrapped with the little guy, but we had also played up to the hilt for him. As we knelt there at his coffin, there wasn't a dry eye when the minister spoke his last words. I cried like a baby."[53]

So did Gehrig. He had lost a mentor.

## NOTES

1. See James A. Cox, *The Lively Ball: Baseball in the Roaring Twenties* (Alexandria, VA: Redefinition Books, 1989).
2. Schoener, *Illustrated History of New York*, 252.
3. Jackson and Dunbar, *Empire City*, 402; and Robinson, *Iron Horse*, 22.
4. Gallico, *Pride of the Yankees*, 79.
5. Lou Gehrig quoted in Bak, *American Classic*, 103.
6. Gehrig and Durso, *My Luke and I*, 128.
7. See Donald Honig, *Baseball's 10 Greatest Teams* (New York: Macmillan, 1982); Lowell Reidenbaugh, *The Sporting News Selects Baseball's 25 Greatest Teams* (St. Louis, MO: The Sporting News, 1988); Harry Hollingsworth, *The Best & Worst Baseball Teams of All Time* (New York: SPI Books, 1994); and Leo Trachtenberg, *The Wonder Team: The True Story of the Incomparable 1927 New York Yankees* (Bowling Green, OH: Bowling Green State University Popular Press, 1995).
8. Gallagher and LaConte, *Yankee Encyclopedia*, 377.
9. Waite Hoyt quoted in Robinson, *Iron Horse*, 106.
10. Miller Huggins quoted in Robinson, *Iron Horse*, 105.
11. Gallagher and LaConte, *Yankee Encyclopedia*, 377–378.
12. Gene Schoor, *The History of the World Series* (New York: William Morrow, 1990), 114–117.
13. Ruth's attempted steal of second convinced some sportswriters that the Yankees had thrown the Series. Huge sums of money had been bet on the Cardinals against a Yankee team that was widely considered invincible. Along with Ruth's faux pas, Bob Meusel didn't hit until Game 6 and Urban Shocker, a 19-game winner that season, pitched horribly twice in the Series, leading the scribes to suspect that the Fall Classic wasn't on the level. See Stout and Johnson, *Yankees Century*, 119.
14. Gallagher and LaConte, *Yankees Encyclopedia*, 377–378.
15. G. H. Fleming, *Murderer's Row: The 1927 New York Yankees* (New York: William Morrow, 1985), 38.
16. Robinson, *Iron Horse*, 107.
17. Gehrig quoted in *New York World*, February 20, 1927.
18. *New York Telegraph*, March 5, 1927.
19. Stout and Johnson, *Yankees Century*, 121.
20. Ibid., 120.
21. Ibid., 121–122.
22. Bill Slocum, "Gehrig Leads HR Race," *New York American*, May 8, 1927.
23. James R. Harrison, *New York Times*, June 24, 1927.
24. Ibid., July 5, 1927.
25. Marshall Hunt, *New York Daily News*, August 18, 1927.
26. William Hennigan, *New York World*, September 14, 1927.

27. Ruth quoted in Robert W. Creamer, *Babe: The Legend Comes to Life* (New York: Simon & Schuster, 1974), 309.

28. Ruth quoted in Robinson, *Iron Horse*, 113–114.

29. Gehrig quoted in Bak, *American Classic*, 71.

30. Bak, *American Classic*, 71.

31. Ibid, 66. Despite Gehrig's impressive totals, many sportswriters believed that Ruth should have won the Most Valuable Player award. But the Bambino, who had already won the honor in 1923, wasn't on the writer's ballot since previous winners were ineligible in those years.

32. Wolff, *Baseball Encyclopedia*, 250–251.

33. Rob Neyer and Eddie Epstein, *Baseball Dynasties: The Greatest Teams of All Time* (New York: W.W. Norton, 2000), 104–105.

34. Lloyd Waner quoted in ibid., 105.

35. Wolff, *Baseball Encyclopedia*, 248.

36. Schoor, *History of the World Series*, 119–122.

37. Neyer and Epstein, *Baseball Dynasties*, 93, 110.

38. Ibid., 94

39. If consistency, or the ability to repeat a pennant-winning performance in three or more seasons, is the mark of baseball excellence, then the 1927 Yankees, whose dynasty spanned the period 1926–1928, do not match the statistical totals of such teams as the 1969–1971 Baltimore Orioles, the 1929–1931 Philadelphia Athletics, or even the 1997–1998 Yankees.

40. See James R. Harrison, "Yanks Sweep Series, Wild Pitch Beating Pirates, 4–3, In Ninth," *New York Times*, October 9, 1927; and H. I. Phillips, "Yanks a Team of Destiny" *New York Sun*, October 10, 1927.

41. Robinson, *Iron Horse*, 120–121.

42. Smelser, *Life that Ruth Built*, 362. See also Yankee payroll figures for 1927 quoted in Edward Barrow to American League Office, Chicago; May 23, 1927, National Baseball Hall of Fame Library. Ruth's salary for the 1927 season amounted to more than 40 percent of the Yankees' total payroll of $170,000 for that season.

43. Creamer, *Babe*, 310.

44. Gallagher and LaConte, *Yankee Encyclopedia*, 380–381; and Stout and Johnson, *Yankees Century*, 135.

45. Schoor, *History of the World Series*, 123–127.

46. Ruth, *Babe Ruth Story*, 162–163.

47. Graham, *Quiet Hero*, 124.

48. Creamer, *Babe*, 324–325.

49. Huggins quoted in Neyer and Epstein, *Baseball Dynasties*, 96.

50. Huggins quoted in Graham, *Quiet Hero*, 128.

51. Graham, *Quiet Hero*, 128.

52. *New York Times*, September 26, 1929.

53. Ruth, *Babe Ruth Story*, 175.

Buster and the Babe, sometime in the late 1920s. *National Baseball Hall of Fame Library, Cooperstown, N.Y.*

5

# BUSTER AND THE BABE, 1929–1934

The death of manager Miller Huggins marked the end of a championship dynasty for the New York Yankees and cast a pall over the club for the next two seasons. Before he died, Huggins was forced to rebuild the team at some positions, realizing that he could not keep pace with the Philadelphia Athletics. Mark Koenig was slipping defensively and was forced to yield to Leo Durocher, a cocky 23-year-old who was given more time at shortstop. An aging Bob Meusel could no longer provide the slugging threat of former years and was platooned in the outfield with Cedric Durst, Sammy Byrd, and Ben Paschal. Thirty-three-year-old catcher Pat Collins had been traded to the Boston Braves and it was clear to Huggins that splitting time between light-hitting holdovers Johnny Grabowski (.203, 0 HR, 2 RBIs) and Benny Bengough (.194, 0 HR, 7 RBIs) was not going to work offensively. Instead, the Mighty Mite inserted 22-year-old Bill Dickey (.324, 10 HR, 65 RBIs) behind the plate, marking the beginning of his seventeen-year Hall of Fame career.

Despite productive performances by Gehrig (.300, 35 HR, 126 RBIs), Ruth (.345, 46 HR, 154 RBIs), and Lazzeri (.354, 18 HR, 106 RBIs), the pitching was unable to carry the club any closer than second place. The ineffectiveness of Pennock (9–11, 49 K, 4.90 ERA) and Hoyt (10–9, 57 K, 4.23 ERA), in particular, hurt the team as the Yanks finished a distant eighteen games behind the powerful A's, who were in the process of forging a championship dynasty of their own.[1] Yankee scout Paul Krichell even began to question whether Gehrig, his own former prospect, should be in the club's future.

During the summer of 1929, Krichell began to show interest in an 18-year-old prospect by the name of Hank Greenberg. Greenberg, a Jew who was born and raised in the Bronx, had recently graduated from James Monroe High School. Although he had demonstrated the ability to hit with power in the local semi-pro leagues, he was a better performer on the basketball court than on the baseball diamond.[2] Still, the Yankees were anxious to sign him because of the potential he had to attract a sizable fan base among the city's Jewish community. Krichell invited the lanky youngster to attend the final game of the regular season between New York and the A's at Yankee Stadium. During the first inning, when Gehrig stepped into the on-deck circle, the scout leaned over and whispered in Greenberg's ear, "He's all washed up. In a few years you'll be the Yankee first baseman."[3] Greenberg wasn't convinced, though. "I heard what Krichell was saying, but it made no impression on me because I was so awed by the sight of Gehrig kneeling in the on-deck circle, only a few feet away," he recalled years later. "His shoulders were a yard wide and his legs looked like mighty oak trees. I'd never seen such sheer brute strength. 'No way I'm going to sign with this team,' I said to myself. 'Not with him playing first base.' I turned to Krichell and said, 'That Lou Gehrig looks like he's got a lot of years left."[4]

Intent on securing Greenberg's services, Krichell pointed out that Gehrig's batting average had slipped from .374 the previous season to just under .300, and offered the youngster a $10,000 bonus to sign.[5] As Greenberg sat in the box seats mulling over the offer, he watched Gehrig lay down bunts in his final two at-bats. Jimmy Dykes, the A's third baseman, didn't bother to make a play on either one. Dykes realized that Gehrig was trying to boost his average to an even .300 for the season, and respectfully yielded to him in a game that meant nothing for either team since the A's had already clinched the pennant. The incident convinced Greenberg that he had no future in the Yankee organization because it would be extremely difficult to replace Gehrig in the hearts and minds of Yankee fans and players, let alone those from other teams.[6]

Gehrig realized that Krichell doubted his ability to rebound from what was a sub par season for him. He knew that other prospects were being courted to succeed him as the Yankee first baseman and he resented their presence in the stands. Lou was never able to forget about the Yankees' interest in Greenberg, who would go on to become a Hall-of-Famer in his own right with Detroit. Just before his death in 1986, the former Tiger slugger discussed the personal grudge Gehrig held against him:

> I was in the American League a year and a half before Gehrig said a word to me. I remember the first time he spoke to me. It was in the middle of the 1934 season, just after we passed the Yankees and

> went into first place. I got a single and was standing on first base. He turned to me and said, sort of gruffly, "Aren't you even going to say hello?"
>
> "Hello, Lou," I said. That's all. I couldn't think of anything else to say. I think I was scared of him. From then on it was just "hello" and that was it. We never chatted.[7]

Gehrig went on to disprove Krichell and the naysayers. In 1930, he hit .379 with 41 home runs and a league-leading 174 runs batted in. During one ten-game streak, Lou collected at least one RBI per game for a total of 27 during the streak. But poor fielding and pitching doomed the Yankees to a third-place finish, sixteen games behind the mighty Athletics.[8] During the season finale at Boston's Fenway Park, Gehrig was asked by Manager Bob Shawkey to play left field so that he could keep utility-man Harry Rice's bat in the line-up. Dutifully, Lou obliged, thereby ending his streak of 885 consecutive games at first base.[9] Gehrig had an even better season in 1931. He hit .341, tied Ruth for the league home-run crown with 46, and set the American League single season RBI record with 184. The performance earned him the *Sporting News*' American League Player of the Year award.[10] But the Yankees, under new manager Joe McCarthy, finished in second once again behind the pennant-winning A's.

The mantle of leadership had been quietly passed from Ruth to Gehrig. Ruth's abilities were fading, although he continued to swing a potent bat, hitting ahead of Gehrig. Lou, on the other hand, was in his prime and capable of carrying the team with his explosive hitting. Most power hitters of the 1930s swung a bat that weighed between 36 and 38 ounces and planted their back foot firmly in the ground while raising their front foot high in the air to trigger their swing. Gehrig, a flat-footed hitter, swung a heavier 40-ounce bat that was 35½ inches long and had a large barrel, medium handle, and small knob. Using his back foot to push off the ground as he began his swing, the Yankee slugger's left knee served as a pivot for the quick rotation of his trunk. His power came not only from his upper body, but also from a contiguous motion that began from his feet and carried through his knees, hips, torso, shoulders, arms, and wrists.[11] Unlike Ruth's long, graceful swing, which drove the ball hard, high, and far, Gehrig's swing was more of a savage attack on the ball and produced line-drive home runs.[12]

"Ruth had that uppercut swing," recalled Charlie Gehringer, the Detroit Tigers' second baseman. "The only thing he'd hit hard would be in the air. I don't even remember him ever hitting a double play ball. He wouldn't hit it hard enough. It'd have that top spin and dribble along. But Gehrig? He'd hammer 'em. His line drives would knock your legs off."[13] Tommy Henrich, a Yankee teammate, agreed. "Lou hit smashes in all directions," he said. "He hit them as hard and as far to left field as to right. And I mean he really smashed them. I've never seen anyone hit line drives like that."[14]

Early in his career Gehrig struck out regularly. But as he learned the strengths and weaknesses of the various opposing pitchers, he reduced his strikeouts from 84 in 1927 to just 31 in 1934. He also became an intelligent hitter who could easily make the adjustments necessary to deliver in the clutch. According to Rick Ferrell, a Hall of Fame catcher who played with the Washington Senators, Boston Red Sox, and St. Louis Browns, there was "no way to pitch to a great hitter like Gehrig. You had to keep moving the ball around the plate. A fast ball here, then maybe call for a change-up. But you couldn't pitch to him the same way every time. He'd adjust and still beat you."[15]

"Ruth got the headlines, but it was Lou who came through for you in the clutch," said Yankee manager Joe McCarthy.[16] Indeed, the consensus around the American League was that Gehrig was a "much more dangerous" hitter than Ruth.[17] Ted Williams of the Boston Red Sox, regarded as the game's greatest hitter, claims that its "difficult to separate Ruth and Gehrig offensively—they were both .340 hitters and both slugged well over .600." What's more, Gehrig was "so great a hitter that he was able to play alongside the most flamboyant figure in the history of American sport and still emerge as a star in his own right."[18] That Gehrig managed to achieve stardom alongside Ruth was also due to the Babe's cultivation of him.

In his early years with the Yankees Gehrig was admittedly "in awe" of the Babe and "kept away from him as much as possible."[19] But the Bambino, who was down to earth, took an interest in the young first baseman. "Babe seemed to like me," recalled Lou. "He made a point of talking to me on the bench between innings and sitting with me on road trips, and after a while my shyness wore off and I got to know him as one of the boys."[20] To be sure, Ruth realized that Gehrig was a "great admirer" and considered him "like a younger brother who was bashful and backward." He also realized that Lou was "timid about mixing with [him]," but Ruth offered his friendship, telling the young first baseman "everything [he] knew about hitting."[21] Gehrig listened and learned. "Lou was fascinated with the Babe, and couldn't help watching him take batting practice," recalled Bob Shawkey, who replaced Huggins as Yankee manager in 1930. "Ruth would be in the batting cage, launching shot after shot over the fence and there was Lou, hand in chin, watching in awe."[22] Gehrig also took his cues from Ruth on the playing field, developing an unyielding competitiveness. During the 1928 World Series against St. Louis, for example, both Lou and the Babe deliberately knocked out two opposing players on the base paths on the very same play. "I gave [second baseman] Frank Frisch all I had and knocked him kicking," recalled Gehrig. "The ball rolled to short centerfield. Ruth had turned third and was headed for the plate and when he got there he bowled over [catcher] Jimmy Wilson. It was dirty baseball, but that's how we played in those days."[23]

Off the field, Ruth could be just as generous to his younger teammate. Unlike the sportswriters who referred to Gehrig as "Columbia Lou" or his Yankee teammates who called him "Biscuit Pants," a reference to his broad backside, the Babe took to calling Lou "Buster" because of his ability to "bust 'em off the outfield fences."[24] During the off-season, Ruth took him fishing and barnstorming. He shared the spotlight with Gehrig, encouraging him to mix with the hundreds of spectators who flocked to local sandlots to see the "Bustin' Babes" and "Larrupin' Lous" play, and even paid him as much as $10,000 for one trip.[25] Ruth's kindness was based, in part, on the realization that Gehrig's dangerous bat protected him in the line-up and allowed him to set a new home run record in 1927. After he retired, the Sultan of Swat admitted that he "didn't think [he] ever would have established that record if it hadn't been for Lou."[26]

Gehrig appreciated Babe's friendship and reciprocated in different ways. He made Ruth a frequent visitor at his home in New Rochelle, where Mom Gehrig indulged the Babe with home-cooked meals. She considered his gargantuan appetite the ultimate compliment and fussed over him, cooking his favorite dishes, especially pigs' knuckles. Ruth, who grew up in an orphanage, considered the special treatment "one of the rare tastes of home life [he] ever had," and gave Mom Gehrig a Chihuahua puppy as a token of his appreciation.[27] Although Lou was a dedicated family man, he agreed to arrange dates for the Babe whenever the Yankees were on the road. When the team returned to New York, Ruth gave Gehrig his date book—which contained the phone numbers of girls in every American League city—so his wife, Claire, wouldn't learn of his extramarital adventures.[28] At the same time, no two individuals could have been more opposite in personality and behavior. Claire Ruth, the Babe's second wife, identified the differences most succinctly:

> Babe wanted to go on the town when he could. Lou wanted to build a home for his folks in the suburbs and get home to them just as soon as the ball game was over. Babe hated authority. Lou accepted it as just and right. Babe loved people. Lou was a loner, his early shyness replaced by suspicion that came with success. Who knows who was right? Surely Babe was ridiculous when he left a ten-dollar tip where fifty cents would have been generous. But Lou's dimes were just as silly.[29]

To be sure, Babe Ruth was both a product as well as a catalyst of the Roaring Twenties. Outgoing and boisterous, the Babe loved being the center of attention. Not only did he revolutionize the game with his home-run hitting, but his personal excesses were also legendary. He indulged himself with the finest clothing, a twelve-cylinder Packard, and an eleven-room suite at the exclusive Ansonia Hotel on New York's Upper West Side. He had a gargantuan appetite and a remarkable capacity for alcohol and tobacco. "I've seen him at midnight, propped up in bed, order six club sandwiches, a platter of pigs' knuckles and a pitcher of beer," Ty Cobb once confirmed. "He'd down all that while smoking a big, black cigar. The next day, if he hit a homer, he'd trot around the bases complaining about gas pains and a bellyache. Then he'd let out a magnificent belch or fart at will."[30]

A big spender known for his womanizing, Ruth also hungered for female affection, most likely because of a neglected youth. Women were eager to please him, and rarely did he ever turn them down. Once, when the Yankees were playing in St. Louis, he announced that he was going to bed with every girl in the local whorehouse that night—and did.[31] On another occasion, after the Yankees had clinched the pennant in Detroit, Ruth rented four hotel rooms with connecting doors and threw an all-night party. Midway through the evening, he stood on a chair with a beer in one hand and a sandwich in the other and announced, "Any girl who doesn't want to fuck can leave now!" Few of them did. On still another occasion, Gehrig discovered him, naked and half-drunk, in a hotel bedroom with two girls. Sitting at the side of the bed, Ruth was sobbing because, after a night of sexual gymnastics, he was now unable to service both of them.[32]

According to teammate Waite Hoyt, Ruth did whatever he pleased, on and off the field. "Babe seemed to believe that his mere presence in the line-up was all he owed to the club," recalled the Yankee pitcher. "He paid no attention to curfew, never took the room assigned to him, and often trotted into the clubhouse just barely in time to make the game."[33] Tired of the all-night carousing and constant breaking of team rules, Miller Huggins was determined to discipline his star player during the 1927 season. Backed by Ruppert and Barrow, the Yankee skipper fined Ruth $5,000 and suspended him for nine days.[34] After Huggins died in 1929, Ruth went to Ruppert and asked to be manager. The Yankee owner replied, "You can't manage yourself, Root! How do you expect to manage others?"[35]

Gehrig, by contrast, was modest and reserved to the point of shyness. He was a devoted family man who worshipped his mother, whom he referred to as his "best girl." He spoiled her with gifts, took her to the best restaurants, and brought her along to spring training for the entire month.[36] Unlike Ruth, who indulged in one-night stands, Gehrig respected women and was somewhat intimidated by them. Once, Lou, hoping to find a permanent female companion, asked two teammates if they knew a "nice girl." The question reduced them to laughter. "You wouldn't know what to do with her if we did!" they replied after managing to collect themselves. On another occasion, some of the more risqué members of the team sent a prostitute up to Gehrig's room, which greatly embarrassed him.[37] Off the field, Lou was a loner. He was not a big drinker, watched carefully what he ate, and was extremely frugal with his money. Instead, he enjoyed the simple pleasures of fishing, skating, and riding the roller coaster at the Rye Beach amusement park.[38]

Extremely sensitive of other people's feelings, Lou rarely engaged in bench jockeying since it discriminated against a player's physical traits or racial or religious background. Nor was it uncommon for him to cry if he felt he had disappointed his manager or teammates. Bob Shawkey, for example, repeatedly warned Gehrig about taking his foot off the first base bag too soon after taking a throw and that sooner or later it would cost the Yankees a close game. When the Yankee manager's prediction came true, Gehrig retreated to the dugout, took a seat at the end of the bench, and "cried like a baby," said Shawkey. "Later on, he came up to my room and apologized, promising that it would never happen again. Lou was that type of person, very sensitive."[39]

Gehrig also took his image as an "All-American hero" to youngsters very seriously. Lou "loved kids," observed Bill Dickey, a teammate and close friend. "He would stand against a rail at the stadium and talk to them all the time."[40] Concerned that his smoking habit would have an adverse effect on youngsters, Gehrig made sure to remove his cigarette or pipe whenever he was photographed.[41] He was "every inch a gentleman" and "the kind of person you'd like your son to be," according to another teammate, Sam Jones.[42] Because Gehrig was a "college man" and "estimable citizen off the playing field," sportswriter Frederick Lieb believed that he was a wonderful role model for "American youth to pattern themselves after." Acknowledging the irony that so many fans "worshipped Babe Ruth for his naughty antics," Lieb wrote that it was refreshing to find "a star athlete with all the virtues generally attributed to sports heroes, but seldom found in them."[43]

Ray Robinson, a 10-year-old Yankee fan, was so enamored of the star first baseman that he wrote him a letter requesting an interview for his school newspaper. Gehrig, true to form, wrote back stating that he would "be happy to talk" with him and to "use this letter to come into the clubhouse." The following day Robinson and a schoolmate were refused entry by a policeman at the clubhouse door, but they decided to sit and wait for their hero. After the game ended, Lou learned of the boys' unfortunate experience. Robinson remembered that Gehrig "seemed genuinely sorry," but was in a hurry to get home. Removing two crumpled tickets from his coat pocket, Lou handed them to his two admirers and asked if they could return another day for the interview.

"Did you really wait all afternoon?" he asked as he stepped into his car, surprised by their devotion.

"Yes," they replied, hoping that he would change his mind and grant the interview.

"I'm really very sorry," he said, and waved good-bye.

More than sixty years later, Robinson recalled Gehrig's "kindness and manner" in the introduction to *Iron Horse*, a biography that he wrote about his childhood hero.[44]

Despite a "puritanical" and "dull" reputation, Gehrig did possess a more raucous side. The Yankee first baseman loved practical jokes and slapstick, and, once in a great while, indulged in sophomoric behavior. Once, he urinated over the terrace of songwriter Fred Fisher's West End Avenue apartment to "break a batting slump."[45] But even at his best—or worst—Gehrig never received the publicity that Ruth did. The Babe overshadowed his younger teammate both on and off the field and yet Gehrig accepted his subordinate position without envy or resentment. "I'm not a headline guy," he once said. "I'm just the guy on the Yankees who's in there every day. I'm the fellow who follows the Babe in the batting order. If I stood on my head, nobody would pay any attention."[46]

As their time together in New York unfolded, the two Yankee stars grew more distant from each other. The first sign of tension in their friendship occurred after the 1929 season when Ruth tried to persuade Gehrig to hold out with him for higher salaries. In January 1930, Yankee owner Jacob Ruppert offered Ruth a two-year contract worth $75,000. The Babe countered with a three-year deal for $85,000. When general manager Ed Barrow refused the demand, Ruth held out until mid-way through spring training when he accepted a two-year deal for $80,000.[47] Despite the fact that the contract made Ruth the highest paid player in the game, the Babe blamed Gehrig for refusing to join him in the holdout, believing that he could have secured more money. But Lou's devotion to the game and his loyalty to the Yankees prevented him from asking for a cent more than the $25,000 management offered to pay him that season.[48] The relationship was further strained by the two players' reception of new manager Joe McCarthy in 1931.

McCarthy never played in the major leagues, but he had gained great respect as the manager of the Chicago Cubs, whom he took to the World Series in 1929. When the Yankees decided not to renew Shawkey's contract at the end of the 1930 season, Barrow, attracted by McCarthy's reputation as a disciplinarian, hired the Chicago skipper as his new manager. Ruth was angered by the decision, believing that he should have been named the Yankee manager. In spring training, he led an anti-McCarthy faction that chafed at the new manager's disciplinary policies, which included a strictly enforced curfew, the wearing of jackets and ties on the road, shaving at home or in the hotel before arriving at the ballpark, and no card playing in the clubhouse.[49] McCarthy was just as demanding of his players on the field.

While most managers viewed spring training games as conditioning exercises for the players, McCarthy wanted to win those contests and had a clear idea of the standard his teams were capable of achieving. After the Yankees crushed the Milwaukee Brewers of the American Association 19–1 in the first exhibition game of the spring, Jimmy Reese, a rookie second baseman, asked McCarthy if he liked the game. "You should have scored thirty runs against a team like that," he snapped.

Gehrig and Dickey, who overheard the exchange, were impressed by their new manager's response. "I like this McCarthy," said Lou.

"So do I," agreed Dickey. "He's our kind of guy."[50]

Gehrig's natural inclination for discipline as well as his genuine respect for McCarthy endeared him to his new manager. He developed a favored-son relationship with McCarthy, and often served as the enforcer of his team policies. Ruth, on the other hand, barely spoke to McCarthy, whom he considered an incompetent manager, and openly questioned his knowledge of the game.[51] During a bridge game that paired Lou and the Babe against some sportswriters, Ruth lost $33 on a wild bid. "Geez, I sure loused that one," he said to the others. "I butchered it like McCarthy handles the pitchers." Gehrig, who believed that such comments should be restricted to the clubhouse, was angered by the remark and later recounted the incident to a teammate, adding that Ruth "has a big, loose mouth" and that he "pops off too damn much about a lot of things."[52] The Babe's dislike of McCarthy served to increase the distance between him and Gehrig. Ruth was also becoming envious of his younger teammate.

When the sportswriters asked the Bambino to name his all-time baseball team later that year, Ruth selected Hal Chase as his first baseman, a purposeful snub of Gehrig.[53] Chase, who played with the Yankees, White Sox, Reds, and Giants between 1905 and 1919, had a career batting average of .291 and a lifetime fielding average of .979.[54] Although Chase's statistical totals were not as good as the .369 batting average and .984 fielding average that Gehrig had compiled in eight major league seasons up to that point in his career, Ruth still defended his choice years later based on Chase's "unbelievable fielding ability."[55] In fact, the Babe's slight can be attributed to the realization that Gehrig's star was rising at precisely the same time his own was in descent. Ruth had already enjoyed his best years in the game by the 1930s and found it increasingly difficult to accept Gehrig as the new leader of the Yankees. That Gehrig emerged as the team's leader in his own right playing alongside Ruth was an outstanding achievement in and of itself.

In 1932, the Yanks captured another pennant and Gehrig enjoyed another impressive year, hitting .349 with 34 home runs and 151 RBIs. His greatest single day in baseball came on June 3 when he hit 4 consecutive home runs against the Philadelphia Athletics and just missed hitting a fifth in the ninth inning of the game.[56] For once, the Babe didn't upstage Lou. Instead, John McGraw stole the spotlight by announcing his retirement from baseball after thirty-one years in the game.[57] Although the 1932 World Series is best remembered for Ruth's "called shot," Gehrig outperformed the Bambino, eliminating any doubt that he was the Yankees' undisputed leader. Lou hit .529 in the four-game World Series, collecting 9 hits, including 3 home runs and a double. He also scored 9 runs and drove in another 8. Ruth, on the other hand, had 5 hits, 2 home runs, and 6 RBIs for a .333 average in his final World Series.[58] Game 3 would prove to be the Babe's swan song.

The Yankees faced the hard-hitting Chicago Cubs in the 1932 Fall Classic. New York won the first two games at home by scores of 12–6 and 5–2, respectively, before the Series moved to Chicago. Prior to the start of Game 3, the jockeying between the two teams was especially intense, much of it focusing on Ruth, who was called "fat," "old," and "nigger" because of his large nose and lips.[59] The Babe actually thrived on the insults, hitting a three-run homer in the first against Cub hurler Charlie Root to give the Yanks an early lead. Gehrig hit a solo shot in the third, but Chicago rallied to tie the game at 4–4 in the fourth inning. Ruth came to bat with the score tied in the top of the fifth and was showered with boos from the Chicago faithful. Leading the jeers was Cub pitcher Guy Bush.

Root delivered the first pitch for a called strike as the crowd cheered and the Cubs razzed the Babe even louder. Ruth, grinning from ear to ear, looked over at the Chicago dugout and raised the index and middle fingers of his right hand, signaling that he had two strikes left. Root's next two deliveries were called balls, but the third one caught the corner of the plate for another called strike. Again, Wrigley Field erupted in a peculiar blend of cheers and jeers. Bush, now standing in front of the Cubs dugout, was screaming at Ruth, who appeared to relish all the pandemonium he had created. This time, the Babe held up just one finger, and shouted to Root on the pitcher's mound, "It only takes one to hit it!"

Gehrig, who was watching the scene from the on-deck circle, later insisted that Ruth told the Cub pitcher that he was "going to knock the next pitch right down his goddamned throat."

Root's next delivery was a change-up, low and away, and the Bambino smashed it deep into the centerfield bleachers for another home run. Ruth circled the bases chortling to himself, "You lucky bum." As he rounded third base, he clasped his hands over his head like a triumphant prize fighter.[60] "Probably no gesture in all the history of baseball was the equal of that," admitted Gehrig, who immediately followed with a home run of his own. "After he hit that home run and ambled around the bases in that peculiar sidling run of his, the place was a madhouse."[61]

The Yankees went on to win the game 7–5 and clinched the Series the following day with a fourth straight win, 13–6. When Joe Williams of the *New York World Telegram* later suggested that Cub pitcher Charley Root purposely allowed Ruth to hit the ball out of the park, Gehrig immediately came to his teammate's defense. "Like hell he did," protested Lou. "Those were low, twisting curves over the outside corner. Any other batter would have been lucky to foul them off. But George gave 'em the works!"[62] True to character, Gehrig continued to keep a low profile, allowing the Babe to bask in the twilight of his final years in the game. Besides, he had discovered another, more refreshing life off the playing field.

During the summer of 1932, Lou began dating Eleanor Twichell, an attractive brunette from Chicago's South Side. Her father, Frank, was a strikingly handsome man who had accumulated a considerable fortune as a concessionaire for the city's five largest parks.[63] A self-described "loner" as a child, Eleanor withdrew into her own world of books, horseback-riding, and ice-skating.[64] After her father began a series of extra-marital affairs, she and her mother tried to compensate for their heartbreak by spending the family's considerable wealth in Chicago's most exclusive stores.[65] By the mid-1920s, Eleanor, a fair-skinned, attractive young lady, was leading a carefree existence. Dividing her time between the golf course, the race track, and local nightclubs, she later admitted:

> I could hold my liquor, even though I was pretty far from being a lush. I don't remember too many days when I missed playing eighteen holes of golf or riding horseback for an hour or two, no matter how late the party had lasted the night before. . . . I got fairly sharp at the race track, too. When I won, I collected; when I lost, I charged it to my father's account. . . . I was well-known in speakeasy society, too.
>
> I suppose that, in the 1920s, you could say I fiddled while Chi-

> cago burned, I was young and rather innocent, but I smoked, played poker, drank bathtub gin along with everybody else, collected $5 a week in allowance from my father, spent $100 a week, made up the difference from winter-book jackpots at the race track that filled a dresser drawer with close to $10,000 at one point, and I learned to become a big tipper.[66]

At the same time, Eleanor was savvy about the opposite sex, circulating with "safely married women as golfing partners by day" and "older, less eager escorts by night."[67] It was during one of these chaperoned outings, in 1928, that the attractive, young socialite was introduced to Lou Gehrig.

Seated in a field box at Comiskey Park with a married friend, Dorothy Grabiner, Eleanor took notice of the muscular Yankee first baseman with handsomely chiseled features. Dorothy, the wife of the White Sox general manager Harry Grabiner, introduced her to Gehrig, who didn't express much of an interest at the time.[68] Things were different when they met again, three years later.

With the stock market crash in 1929, the nation was mired in the Great Depression and Frank Twichell's fortune was destroyed. Eleanor went to work as a $40-a-week secretary at the "Century of Progress" fairgrounds where Chicago was planning to host the 1932 World's Fair. She had also put her party-going ways behind her to spend her evenings reading good literature.[69] One day after work, a friend invited Eleanor to her apartment to "meet Lou" and she accepted. That evening Gehrig monopolized her time, giving Eleanor "a shy man's version of the rush."[70]

"Handsome," she thought. "Big, handsome—6 feet tall, about 200 pounds—sturdy as a rock and innocent as a waif."[71] Lou walked her home that night and left her abruptly at the door to her apartment without so much as a good night kiss. But a week later, he sent her a diamond cut–crystal necklace. They dated steadily for the next nine months until the Yankees' first trip to Chicago in the spring of 1933, when he proposed over breakfast at the Drake Hotel.[72]

Lou told Eleanor that his mother, who had been the sole object of his affections, "would be hard to handle."[73] His prediction soon came true. After traveling to Chicago to meet her future daughter-in-law, Mom Gehrig flatly rejected her, just as she had done with every other woman in which her son expressed a romantic interest. She told Lou that Eleanor was a "high society girl" who "wouldn't be able to care for [him]."[74] Shortly after, the Yankee slugger confided his disappointment to sportswriter Fred Lieb. "Mom is the most wonderful woman in the world," he admitted. "She broke up some of my earlier romances, but she isn't going to break this one."[75]

In September, Eleanor left for New York to find an apartment for the couple. She hoped to move close enough to the Gehrig's New Rochelle home to "make the parting of mother and son less sorrowful," but distant enough to maintain her and Lou's privacy.[76] When Mom Gehrig insisted that the couple share their house where she could continue to care for her son, Lou told her that "from the day of my marriage, Eleanor will come first" and that he had "no intention of doubling up with [his] parents."[77] Heartbroken, Mom Gehrig threatened to boycott the wedding, which was scheduled for later that month at the Long Island home of Eleanor's relatives. Lou had heard enough.

On September 28, the day before the wedding, he phoned the mayor of New Rochelle, a lawyer named Walter G. C. Otto, and had him conduct the marriage at the couple's unfinished apartment in New Rochelle. Afterwards, a contingent of policemen on motorcycles escorted the groom to Yankee Stadium so he could preserve his unbroken streak of games. The following day, a small reception was held for the couple at the Long Island home of Eleanor's aunt and uncle. Sportswriter Fred Lieb brought Mom Gehrig with him and, to Lou's surprise, she behaved herself.[78] Conspicuously absent, however, was Babe Ruth, who had not been invited.[79] When the sportswriters asked Lou if there had been a falling out between the two players, he denied any ill feelings on his part. "Babe's my pal," he insisted. "We aren't fighting with each other. We've always fought together for the good of the ball club."[80] In fact, the two players struggled to tolerate each other.

A serious breach in their relationship came sometime during the 1933 season when Ruth visited the Gehrig home in New Rochelle along with his daughter Dorothy. The 12-year-old girl, a child from his first marriage, behaved and dressed like a tomboy; nothing like her step-sister Julia, who, at 18 years old, was a fashionably dressed young lady. Mom Gehrig immediately noted the difference between the two daughters. "It's a shame that Claire [Ruth's second wife] doesn't dress Dorothy as nicely as she dresses her own daughter," she remarked to another guest. When Claire heard about Mom Gehrig's observation she was furious, which, in turn, angered the Babe. Ruth went directly to Gehrig and demanded that his mother "mind her own business." Naturally, Lou, who adored his mother, stopped speaking to his teammate and Ruth reciprocated.[81] The incident ended a once-inseparable relationship. In front of the cameras, the two men pretended friendship, but even that was difficult. Film clips still exist of Ruth crossing the plate after hitting a home run and Gehrig turning conveniently away from him to say something to the bat boy or another teammate, anything to avoid greeting Ruth.

"The problem wasn't really between Daddy and Lou as much as it was between mother and Mom Gehrig," insists Julia Ruth Stevens, the Babe's step-daughter. "When Dorothy visited Mom Gehrig she was wearing some clothes that were rather plain, they might have even been torn. Mom Gehrig was horrified. She said some things that got back to mother, who told Daddy about it. Daddy got angry and told Lou to tell his mother to mind her own business. It was all so stupid. It's really very sad that what was once a great friendship between Daddy and Lou had to break up over something like that."[82]

Lou initiated friendships with other, younger teammates with personalities similar to his own. Among the players to whom he endeared himself was Bill Dickey, a quiet young catcher from Arkansas. When Dickey was first promoted to the Yankees he was pressing and found himself in a batting slump. Gehrig encouraged him, studied his swing, and helped him correct his hitting mechanics. "If Lou hadn't done that for me, the chances are that nobody else would have bothered and I might have been kicking around in some tank town league, or out of baseball altogether," Dickey confessed. "He was always doing something for rookies. Without even being asked, he'd study their mistakes, and explain just how to correct them."[83] Gehrig and Dickey quickly became close friends and could often be found playing cards together or fishing during the off-season. Both were also highly principled individuals who attached a greater importance to their marriages than most other ballplayers.[84]

Another kindred spirit was Frank Crosetti. Gehrig took the shy, 21-year-old rookie under his wing in 1932 and taught him how to adjust to life in the majors. "Lou didn't like people who bragged," said Crosetti. "I think that's why he took a liking to me. I was very quiet. Lou made me feel like I belonged. On game days he'd pick me up, drive me to the ball park, and after the game, drop me off back at the hotel."[85] The only exception to these silent types was Lefty Gomez, a lanky pitcher who loved to wisecrack opponents and teammates alike. Gehrig was attracted to Gomez because of his free-spiritedness and his uncanny ability to lessen the demands of the game through his clubhouse antics.[86]

While Gehrig's newfound friendships eased the burdens of his professional life, Eleanor opened new avenues for self-discovery in his personal life. She introduced him to the opera and ballet, activities that were spurned by ballplayers. Lou insisted that the couple attend performances secretly so he wouldn't have to endure the heckling of teammates. At the same time, however, he was deeply moved by them. Eleanor quickly discovered that her husband was a gentle, sensitive man who was "shaken to tears" by *Tristan und Isolde*, an opera about two lovers who discover each other too late in life and achieve happiness only in death. Lou was also known to weep while Eleanor read him *Anna Karenina*.[87] "These experiences were new to him," she explained, "but the feelings had been deep inside, waiting for the masterwork that might bring them out. That's the way he was—anything he loved, he embraced to the point of tears, and it was that way in every direction he turned."[88]

Eleanor had won over Lou's affections so completely that he even placed her above his own mother. That is not to say that he ignored his parents or their needs. After he married, Lou placed all his life's savings into a trust fund for them, providing for himself and Eleanor by banking his regular season salary, World Series bonus money, and endorsement checks.[89] He also gave his parents the deed to the house at 9 Meadow Lane in New Rochelle. While Lou made sure that he and Eleanor lived in an apartment just as few blocks away at 5 Circuit Road, he made clear to his mother that his wife "came first."[90] To underscore the point, Lou took Mom Gehrig to see Sidney Howard's *The Silver Lord*, a drama about a domineering mother who constantly interfered in her son's marriage.[91] Fortunately, Mom Gehrig got the message and respected Lou's wishes. Eleanor still had to share Lou with baseball, though.

After their marriage, the couple agreed that Lou would retire from the game when he reached the age of 35. He was already 30 years old at the time, but neither of them wanted to live through the embarrassment endured by a fading star.[92] Despite their mutual understanding about retirement and the financial security he enjoyed, Lou still worried about his performance. When the Yankees lost a game, he played it over and over again in his mind, wondering how he might have created a more favorable outcome. Sometimes, during these periods of self-rebuke, Lou would exile himself to another room, refusing to speak with Eleanor for hours. Nothing she did could snap him out of it.[93] Even during the best of times, when Lou was performing at the top of his game, he wondered just how much longer the Yankees would keep him on their payroll; this was one of the reasons he was so quick to sign whatever salary offers the team made to him. "No matter what his achievements, Lou was dogged by a sense of failure and a need, constantly, to prove himself," said Eleanor, after his death. "Success brought Lou no sense of attainment, no relaxation. It was like something ephemeral to be clutched with both hands. He was afraid if he loosened his grip for a moment, everything he had struggled for would slip away."[94] But Gehrig's career was far from over in 1933.

Although age had caught up with the Yankees that season as New York dropped to second place seven games behind the Washington Senators, the team still had a solid nucleus. With Ruth (.301, 34 HR, 103 RBIs), Combs (.298, 5 HR, 60 RBIs), and Sewell (.273, 2 HR, 54 RBIs) in decline, a younger generation of hitters was emerging. Gehrig (.334, 32 HR, 139 RBIs) was the offensive star of the team, but Lazzeri (.294, 18 HR, 104 RBIs) and Dickey (.318, 14 HR, 97 RBIs) also enjoyed productive seasons, while Gomez (16–10, 163 K, 3.18 ERA) emerged as the new ace of the pitching staff.[95] What's more, Gehrig was beginning to forge his own legend by breaking the major league record for most consecutive games played. On August 17, Lou broke the previous record of 1,307 straight games held by former Yankee shortstop Everett Scott. The game, played at St. Louis' Sportsman's Park, was interrupted after the first inning so American League president Will Harridge could present Gehrig with a silver statuette marking the occasion. Although the Yanks lost that day, Gehrig, who collected two hits, was dubbed the "Iron Horse" of baseball by sportswriters.[96]

The 1934 season proved to be even better for Lou. He became the first Yankee ever to win the coveted Triple Crown for leading the American League in the three top offensive categories, with a .363 batting average, 49 home runs, and 165 RBIs.[97] He also hit 4 grand slams and 30 home runs at Yankee Stadium that season, setting new club records.[98] On two occasions, however, Gehrig's continuous game streak almost ended. The first incident came during an exhibition game against the Newark Bears on June 29 when Lou was beaned by Ray White, a young Yankee farm hand. White hit Gehrig in the head with a fastball, knocking him out cold for five minutes. When he was revived, Lou was rushed to the hospital where doctors said he suffered a bad concussion. Although they insisted that the Yankee slugger stay off the ball field for a few days, the Iron Horse refused. The next day he insisted on playing against Washington, despite a severe headache. He went 3-for-3 in that game, hitting three triples before the contest was rained out in the fifth inning.[99]

Two weeks later, on July 13 in Detroit, Gehrig felt a sharp pain in his back during the second inning, while running out a base hit. The pain left him doubled over at first base, but he refused to leave the game until he realized that he couldn't bend down to field his position. Still laboring with a stiff back the next day, Gehrig asked McCarthy to insert him in the lead-off spot so he could preserve the streak. The Yankee manager obliged, penciling his star into the line-up as the lead-off hitter and shortstop. Gehrig somehow managed to get a base hit and was then replaced by Red Rolfe, who came in to pinch run and play shortstop.[100] The incident earned Gehrig some harsh press.

"Instead of enhancing his reputation for durability, Gehrig sullied it," wrote Bud Shaver of the *Detroit Times*. "He also impugned his reputation for sensibility. If a man is too ill to play, the sensible thing for him to do is refrain from playing. His physical handicaps are apt to be disastrous for his teammates. Records preserved in the manner in which Gehrig preserved his at Navin Field prove nothing but the absurdity of most records."[101] Dan Daniel of the *New York World Telegram* was a bit more objective. After the game, the New York scribe asked Lou if he wasn't being foolish to play just to preserve his streak. "I don't believe in making a practice of that sort of thing," replied Gehrig. "I don't want to cheapen the record. If I can't play through, we'll let it lapse."[102]

Another sportswriter, James M. Kahn of the *New York Sun*, remembered the excruciating pain that Gehrig experienced in the July 13 game and began to note similar attacks over the next few seasons. While Gehrig and the Yankees dismissed these incidents as "lumbago" or a "back cold," Kahn wrote that the attacks "escaped accurate diagnosis," but made it "painful and difficult for Gehrig to breathe until they wore off in a couple of days."[103] It may have been an early sign of amyotrophic lateral sclerosis.

After the 1934 season ended, Lou and Eleanor joined Connie Mack and fourteen other major leaguers on a tour of Japan, where baseball was becoming increasingly popular. Mack asked Babe Ruth, who was accompanied by his wife Claire and her daughter Julia, to serve as field manager, while he would assume the duties of a general manager for the squad. In fact, the legendary A's manager was using the tour, in part, as an opportunity to see if Ruth could actually manage a team and, if so, succeed him in Philadelphia. It seemed like an easy job, considering the tremendous talent on the team. Among the players were pitchers Lefty Gomez, Earl Whitehill, Clint Brown, and Joe Cascarella; catchers Charlie Berry and Moe Berg; infielders Gehrig, Jimmie Foxx, Charlie Gehringer, Rabbit Warstler, and Eric McNair; and outfielders, Ruth, Earl Averill, and Bing Miller.[104] But the tension that already existed between Ruth and Gehrig divided the team into factions.

On the voyage across the Pacific, Julia Ruth saw Lou walking on deck and snubbed him by turning in the opposite direction. "Don't stop," she told him. "The Ruths don't speak to the Gehrig's."[105] A few days later, Eleanor accepted an invitation from Claire Ruth to visit with her and the Babe in their cabin. She neglected to tell Lou about her plans and was gone for more than two hours. When Gehrig couldn't find her, he worried that she had fallen overboard and had the ship's crew launch a massive search.

Ruth tried to reconcile with Gehrig but was rebuffed.[106] Matters worsened after the ship docked in the Orient. Lou and Earl Whitehill arrived late to a morning ceremony and Ruth, ironically, threatened to send them both back to the United States if they were late again.[107] Although the tour was a success by most accounts—the Americans playing to sell-out crowds throughout their seventeen-game tour—Ruth's poor relationship with Gehrig and his tendency to defer to his wife convinced Mack that he could never manage in the major leagues. Nor did McCarthy want him on the Yankees any longer. Barrow, who had tired of Ruth's constant efforts to undermine his manager's authority, released the Babe so he could sign with the Boston Braves of the National League.

Shortly after Ruth quit baseball for good in May 1935, Gehrig was asked by the sportswriters whom he considered to be the greatest player of all time. If they anticipated Lou's answer to be Babe Ruth, they must have been sorely disappointed when he replied, "Honus Wagner." When asked why Wagner was a better player than Ruth, Gehrig replied, "Wagner did a great job without any thought of himself. He was the team player of all time."[108]

Not only had Gehrig returned Ruth's snub of his abilities as a first baseman, but he had also completed the painful and bitter divorce that had played out over the course of the previous two years.

## NOTES

1. David S. Neft et al., *The Sports Encyclopedia: Baseball* (New York: Grosset & Dunlap, 1974), 170.

2. Hank Greenberg with Ira Berkow, *Hank Greenberg: The Story of My Life* (New York: Times Books, 1989), 9–13.

3. Paul Krichell quoted in Lawrence S. Ritter, *The Glory of Their Times: The Story of the Early Days of Baseball Told by the Men Who Played It* (New York: Vintage, 1985), 310.

4. Greenberg, *Story of My Life*, 17.

5. Ibid., 18.

6. Ibid., 17–18.

7. Greenberg quoted in Ritter, *Glory of Their Times*, 319.

8. Gallagher and LaConte, *Yankee Encyclopedia*, 382.

9. Bak, *American Classic*, 152.

10. Gallagher and LaConte, *Yankee Encyclopedia*, 382.

11. Bak, *American Classic*, 80.

12. Honig, *Power Hitters*, 35.

13. Charlie Gehringer quoted in Bak, *American Classic*, 54, 56.

14. Tommy Henrich quoted in Honig, *Power Hitters*, 35.

15. Rick Ferrell quoted in Bak, *American Classic*, 83.

16. Joe McCarthy quoted in Bob Kuenster, "These Are Majors' Ten Best First Basemen of All Time," *Baseball Digest*, July 1994, 65.

17. For those who considered Gehrig a tougher out that Ruth, see Jimmie Foxx quoted in Gallagher and LaConte, *Yankee Encyclopedia*, 102; Lefty Grove quoted in Honig, *Power Hitters*, 33; Mel Harder quoted in Bob Dolgan, "Iron Man Lou Gehrig Played in the Shadow of Babe Ruth," *Baseball Digest*, November 1995, 76; and Dan Howley quoted in *New York Sun*, May 13, 1927.

18. Ted Williams and Jim Prime, *Ted Williams' Hit List* (Indianapolis, IN: Masters Press, 1996), 65–66. Williams ranked Ruth and Gehrig as the top two batsmen in the history of the game. Calculating the two players' performances on the basis of offensive "production,"—the sum of on-base percentage and slugging percentage—Williams assigned Ruth a 1.163 ranking and Gehrig a 1.080 ranking. See Williams, *Hit List*, 56–57.

19. Lou Gehrig, "Am I Jealous of Babe Ruth?" 1933, 43. Gehrig Files, National Baseball Hall of Fame Library.

20. Ibid.
21. Ruth, *Babe Ruth Story*, 125, 143.
22. Bob Shawkey quoted in Honig, *Power Hitters*, 35.
23. Gehrig quoted in Bak, *American Classic*, 84.
24. Ruth, *Babe Ruth Story*, 125; Bak, *American Classic*, 54; and Holtje, "Lou Gehrig," 381.
25. Creamer, *Babe*, 379.
26. Ruth, *Babe Ruth Story*, 152.
27. Ibid., 166–167.
28. Gallico, *Pride of the Yankees*, 95; and Pollack interview.
29. Claire Ruth quoted in Bak, *American Classic*, 54.
30. Ty Cobb quoted in Creamer, *Babe*, 320.
31. Creamer, *Babe*, 320.
32. Ibid., 321–322.
33. Hoyt quoted in ibid., 334.
34. Gallagher and LaConte, *Yankee Encyclopedia*, 332.
35. Ruppert quoted in ibid., 333.
36. See Gehrig, "Am I Jealous of Babe Ruth?" 41; Bak, *American Classic*, 107; and Graham, *Quiet Hero*, 159.
37. Bak, *American Classic*, 72.
38. Gehrig and Durso, *My Luke and I*, 138; and Gallico, *Pride of the Yankees*, 100–101.
39. Bob Shawkey quoted in Bak, *American Classic*, 85.
40. Bill Dickey quoted in Maury Allen, *Where Have You Gone, Joe DiMaggio? The Story of America's Last Hero* (New York: Dutton, 1975), 62.
41. Smelser, *Life That Ruth Built*, 329.
42. Sam Jones quoted in Ritter, *Glory of Their Times*, 245.
43. Frederick Lieb, *New York Post*, July 1, 1927.
44. Robinson, *Iron Horse*, 9–15.
45. Ibid., 23.
46. Gehrig quoted in ibid., 125.
47. Smelser, *Life That Ruth Built*, 410.
48. Ibid., 412. Only Ruth, who earned $80,000, Rogers Hornsby, player-manager of the Cubs ($40,000), Hack Wilson of the Cubs ($33,000), and Al Simmons of the A's ($30,000) made more money than Gehrig in 1931.
49. Gallagher and LaConte, *Yankee Encyclopedia*, 381; Creamer, *Babe*, 351–352.
50. Graham, *Quiet Hero*, 144.
51. Bak, *American Classic*, 112.
52. Smelser, *Life that Ruth Built*, 478–479.
53. Ibid., 430.
54. See Martin Donell Kohout, *Hal Chase: The Defiant Life and Turbulent Times of Baseball's Biggest Crook* (Jefferson, NC: McFarland, 2001).
55. Ruth, *Babe Ruth Story*, 223.

56. Bak, *American Classic*, 91–92.
57. Gallagher and LaConte, *Yankee Encyclopedia*, 102.
58. Wolff, *Baseball Encyclopedia*, 2657.
59. Robinson, *Iron Horse*, 24–25. The animosity between the Yankees and Cubs involved the Chicago shortstop, Mark Koenig. Koenig, a former Yankee, had been traded to the Cubs in August 1932 and helped lead Chicago to the National League pennant with his brilliant defense and .353 average. Despite his contribution, his Cub teammates only voted him a half-share of their Series money. The Yankees called the Cubs "cheapskates" for failing to reward their former teammate.
60. Creamer, Babe, 358–365.
61. Gehrig, "Am I Jealous of Babe Ruth?" 41–42.
62. Lou Gehrig quoted in Joe Williams, "Damon and Pythias," *New York World Telegram*, December 8, 1932.
63. Gehrig and Durso, *My Luke and I*, 52.
64. Ibid., 56.
65. Ibid., 61–63.
66. Ibid., 77–78, 94.
67. Ibid., 95.
68. Ibid., 76–77; and Bak, *American Classic*, 117.
69. Gehrig and Durso, *My Luke and I*, 115.
70. Ibid., 135.
71. Ibid., 125.
72. Ibid., 139–140.
73. Lou Gehrig quoted in ibid., 140.
74. Bak, *American Classic*, 119.
75. Lou Gehrig quoted in ibid.
76. Gehrig and Durso, *My Luke and I*, 141.
77. Lou Gehrig quoted in ibid., 160.
78. Bak, *American Classic*, 121.
79. Smelser, *Life That Ruth Built*, 479.
80. Gehrig, "Am I Jealous of Babe Ruth?" 41.
81. Creamer, *Babe*, 379; Smelser, *Life that Ruth Built*, 478–479; and Ray Robinson, "Ruth & Gehrig: Friction Between Gods," *New York Times*, June 2, 1991.
82. Julia Ruth Stevens quoted in ESPN Classics, *Sports Century: Lou Gehrig*.
83. Bill Dickey quoted in Gallico, *Pride of Yankees*, 4–7.
84. Bak, *American Classic*, 108.
85. Frank Crosetti quoted in ibid., 106.
86. Bak, *American Classic*, 108–109.
87. Gehrig and Durso, *My Luke and I*, 26–27.
88. Ibid., 164–165.
89. Bak, *American Classic*, 143.
90. Gehrig and Durso, *My Luke and I*, 159.
91. Ibid., 160.

92. Ibid., 167.

93. Ibid., 166.

94. Eleanor Gehrig quoted in Bak, *American Classic*, 38.

95. Wolff, *Baseball Encyclopedia*, 274–275.

96. "Gehrig Eclipses Scott's Record Playing 1,308th Straight Game," *New York Times*, August 18, 1933.

97. "Gehrig Wins Triple Honors," *Sporting News*, December 6, 1934.

98. Gallagher and LaConte, *Yankee Encyclopedia*, 386. Interestingly, Detroit's Mickey Cochrane was chosen the American League's MVP in 1934. While Cochrane led the Tigers to the American League pennant as player-manager, his offensive totals (.320, 2 HR, 76 RBIs) could hardly compare with Gehrig's.

99. "Gehrig Hitting Maniac Since 'Beaning,' " *New York World Telegram*, August 6, 1934.

100. Bak, *American Classic*, 136.

101. *Detroit Times*, July 15, 1934.

102. Lou Gehrig quoted in Dan Daniel, "Daniel's Dope," *New York World Telegram*, February 11, 1937.

103. Graham, *Quiet Hero*, 175–176.

104. Creamer, *Babe*, 378.

105. Ibid.

106. Gehrig and Durso, *My Luke and I*, 189–190. Eleanor Gehrig downplayed the event as an innocent misunderstanding. But rumors circulated that the Babe, drunk on champagne, tried to seduce her in the presence of his wife. See Bak, *American Classic*, 122–123.

107. Creamer, *Babe*, 379.

108. Lou Gehrig quoted in *New York World Telegram*, May 21, 1935.

The "Iron Horse" at bat. *The Sporting News.*

# 6

# Pride of the Yankees, 1935–1938

In 1935 Lou Gehrig emerged as the Yankees' uncontested leader. With Ruth gone, Lou's friends urged him to assert himself more. Having won the coveted Triple Crown the previous year, Gehrig's credibility was impeccable, although his $30,000 salary was $50,000 less than the Babe received in his peak year.[1] But the Yankees rewarded Lou in other ways.

Manager Joe McCarthy appointed his slugging first baseman team captain, the first Yankee to enjoy that honor since Everett Scott. Lou was flattered by the honor and created more responsibility for himself than simply presenting the line-up card to the umpires before games. In his own quiet way, he enforced McCarthy's policies on personal decorum in the clubhouse and on the playing field. In the process, Gehrig cultivated a special "Yankee mystique" characterized by gentlemanly behavior, a businesslike manner informed by a quiet confidence in self and teammates, and a touch of class that went unmatched in major league baseball.

Those who were fortunate enough to play for the Yankees during those years considered it a privilege to don the dark blue pinstripes. "I was in awe when I first came up to the ball club," recalled Tommy Henrich, who was promoted to New York as a 23-year-old outfielder. "They were polite. They said, 'Good luck, Tom. Nice to meet you.' And then they went back to whatever it was they were doing. The atmosphere in that clubhouse was absolutely that of nine guys getting ready to go out and play ball. And I'll tell 'ya, it was a joy to play with that type of team."[2]

The 1935 Yankees also showed promise on the field. Rookie George Selkirk

(.312, 11 HR, 94 RBIs) replaced Ruth in right field. Red Rolfe, another rookie, became the regular third baseman and hit .300. The pitching was more consistent than it had been in the previous two seasons. Red Ruffing led the team with a 16–11 record and 3.12 ERA and was joined by 25-year-old Johnny Broaca (15–7, 78 K, 3.58 ERA). Johnny Allen (13–6, 113 K, 3.61 ERA), Johnny Murphy (10–5), and Vito Tamulis (10–5) also performed well. Only Lefty Gomez had a disappointing season, posting a 12–15 record. Although Gehrig had another splendid year (.329, 30 HR, 119 RBIs), he was the team's only legitimate power hitter and one who tended to hit in streaks.[3] As much as he tried, the Iron Horse couldn't carry the team by himself. "Lou would go for days hitting line drive after line drive," said Bill Dickey. "He probably hit a ball harder in every direction than any man who ever played. Then suddenly he would stop, for no reason."[4] When the Yanks finished second for the third straight season, general manager Ed Barrow realized that he had to find another power hitter to compliment Gehrig. That slugger was a 21-year-old outfielder named Joe DiMaggio.

DiMaggio gained national attention two years earlier when he batted safely in 61 consecutive games for the San Francisco Seals of the Pacific Coast League. He completed the 1933 season with a .340 batting average, 28 home runs, and a league-leading 168 RBIs.[5] Scouts raved about his natural talent, some claiming that he was the best all-around player they had ever seen. Their interest declined, however, when the young outfielder hurt a knee in 1934. But the Yankees, who originally offered the Seals $75,000 for DiMaggio's services, paid $25,000 for the injured outfielder and allowed him to play with San Francisco for one more season before bringing him to New York.[6]

Like Gehrig, DiMaggio was shy when he first came up to the Yankees, but he also had a certain magnetism and self-assurance about him. On the first day of spring training camp in 1936, Lou walked over to the rookie as he was being introduced to the team by McCarthy, extended his hand, and quietly said, "Nice to have you with us, Joe." DiMaggio just nodded.[7] Despite his low-key disposition, the New York sportswriters quickly anointed the prospect "Babe's successor." Dan Daniel of the *New York World Telegram* took one look at DiMaggio at batting practice and wrote, "Here is the replacement for Babe Ruth."[8] Similarly, after DiMaggio paced the Yankees to a 14–5 rout of the lowly St. Louis Browns in early May, Don Hallman of the *New York Daily News* wrote, "Now the cheers of New York fans are not handed out to every fellow. In fact, they have subsided almost to a whisper since Babe Ruth packed his duds and went through the gates. But yesterday they rolled in happy volume across the field and back again for a rookie stepping up to fill the vacant shoes of Big Boy Ruth."[9] Within a year's time, Ruth would agree. When Jimmy

Powers of the *New York Daily News* asked the Babe in a 1937 interview to "pick his successor," the Bambino replied, "This DiMaggio boy sure looks like a natural to become the number one hitter in the game."[10]

The Yankee players were also smitten with DiMaggio. From the start he was part of the clubhouse camraderie. When his teammates teased him about his Italian heritage calling him "Dago," the young outfielder accepted it in such a good natured way that the name became a term of endearment. "Joe seemed to fit in with the guys right away," said outfielder George Selkirk. "He played a little bridge and he was good natured about being kidded. He also proved to be the big guy we were looking for, the home run guy. We needed a leader after Ruth left. Gehrig wasn't it. He was just a good old plough horse. But after Joe D joined the ball club we started winning pretty regularly."[11] Once again, Gehrig found himself in the shadows of another star. The irony wasn't lost on Lefty Gomez, who had mixed emotions about DiMaggio's ascendancy:

> Joe became a big star almost as soon as he joined the Yankees. The man I felt sorry for was Lou Gehrig. He had always played behind Ruth and finally Ruth quit and he had it all to himself in 1935. Now in '36 Joe comes along. Lou had another big year but Joe was a rookie sensation so he got all the attention.
>
> The relationship between Joe and Lou was very good. They never had a cross word that I know of. They were both quiet fellows and they got along. But it just seemed a shame that Lou never got the attention he deserved. He didn't seem to care, but maybe he did. Anyway, I always felt a little sorry for him because of it.[12]

If Gehrig resented DiMaggio, he didn't show it. Lou's dedication to the game and concern for the team seemed to take precedence over any feelings of jealousy he might have harbored toward the budding star. In fact, Gehrig defended DiMaggio in one of his first games as a Yankee, earning the rookie's gratitude. During that occasion, umpire George Moriarity tried to humble the young outfielder by calling two questionable pitches strikes. When DiMaggio turned around and glared at him as if to question the calls, Moriority snapped, "Turn around!" Gehrig, who was kneeling on the on-deck circle, shouted out, "Leave the kid alone, George! If you call 'em right, he won't have to turn around."[13]

Ray Robinson believes Gehrig's "profound sense of himself as a public figure" and "self-designated role as a loyal team player" enabled him to find great "contentment with his role as Yankee captain."[14] Nothing else mattered more than those personal commitments, with the possible exception of his individual performance on the diamond.

Gehrig, who experienced a lot of difficulty playing first base early in his career, now took great pride in his ability to play the position. "In the beginning, I used to make one terrible play a game," he confessed to Quentin Reynolds of *Sport Magazine*, looking back at his rookie year. "Then I got so I'd make one a week, and finally I'd pull a bad one about once a month. Now, I'm trying to keep it down to one a season."[15]

With DiMaggio and Gehrig as their third and fourth hitters, respectively, the Yankees won the American League pennant in 1936 by 19½ games and went on to defeat the New York Giants in the World Series, 4 games to 2. Gehrig's productivity improved with DiMaggio's bat in the line-up. Joe D hit .323 with 29 home runs and 125 RBIs. Lou was even better, compiling a .354 batting average, 49 homers, and 152 RBIs. The Iron Horse also led the league in slugging (.696), runs scored (167), and walks (130). What's more, Gehrig was, for the first time in his career, the undisputed home-run king and was voted most valuable player by the *Sporting News*.[16]

But the greatest thrill of his baseball career came in the third inning of Game 4 of the 1936 World Series when he hit a two-run homer off of another future Hall-of-Famer, Carl Hubbell of the Giants. "We had a 2–1 lead in games at that point," remembered Gehrig. "Had Hubbell beaten us that day and tied up the Series we would have been in a tough spot. But that two-run homer of mine clinched the game and, I felt, the championship. That was my biggest thrill because you don't hit against very many pitchers like Hubbell in a lifetime, and you don't hit very many homers off the Hubbells in such situations."[17]

Indeed, Lou Gehrig had everything he wanted in life by 1937. His success on the ball diamond was only surpassed by the happiness of his marriage to Eleanor. She gave him the personal reassurance he needed by building his self-esteem, managed the household, and took part in his favorite activities of fishing and ice skating. While most couples quarreled over money, Lou trusted Eleanor completely with their financial welfare. In fact, he handed over the checkbook and savings account to her shortly after their marriage with the words, "Our old age is in your hands now." Never did he question Eleanor's bills, and rarely did he spend money on anything for himself.[18] Their marriage was based on a deep respect for each other and an abiding friendship. Accordingly, Lou considered Eleanor his "pal," a term of endearment he regularly used, and she, in a fun-loving way, considered him a "huge but proper wallflower."[19] Once, as a testimony of her love, Eleanor collaborated with a professional songwriter, Fred Fisher, on a song titled "I Can't Get to First Base with You" and dedicated it to her husband.[20] But it was their daily routine that endeared them to each other.

During the season Eleanor would awaken Lou at 10:00 A.M. and make him a large breakfast of bacon, eggs, wheat cakes, fruit, and a single cup of coffee. At noon they left for the ballpark together. After the game they returned home for dinner; rarely did they dine out during the season. Sometimes dinner was followed by a movie or a concert, but usually the couple remained at home to enjoy an evening of reading, listening to classical music, or playful wrestling with each other.[21] If they shared a weakness, it was chain-smoking. Ironically, for as much as Lou watched his diet, eating two large but balanced meals a day and avoiding sweets, he was constantly smoking cigarettes or, at home, a pipe. Eleanor was just as bad, "sneaking one cigarette after another," probably as a way to maintain her comely figure.[22] Despite the indiscretion, Lou was in wonderful shape.

In 1936, when physicians at Columbia University Medical College examined him, they found that Gehrig had a small heart. His heart rate of seventy-two beats per minute was "characteristic of athletes with great endurance." After strenuous exercise, Lou's heart rate returned to normal in ninety seconds. His blood pressure was an ideal 126 over 82, and his reflexes were perfect.[23] With such a clean bill of health, Gehrig anticipated more than a few productive years as a player, and hoped to manage afterwards. Since McCarthy's contract was due to expire soon, rumors began to circulate that the Iron Horse would succeed him as a player-manager. But because of his strong respect for the Yankee skipper, Lou publicly stated his intention to pursue that goal "somewhere else."[24] For the time being, however, Gehrig's attentions were focused on the team's potential to return to the Fall Classic and his own consecutive game streak.

On the eve of the 1937 season, Lou announced his five-year plan. "I've played in 1,808 games and hope to stretch the string to 2,500," he told the New York press. "Some people think I'm crazy to play day in and day out. But I know myself better than other people know me. I get enough days off during the season to prevent going stale. I am only thirty-three, and I don't have to begin worrying about my legs—not just yet." At the same time, the Iron Horse promised that he would "not endanger the success of the ball club by sticking in the line-up if he was not fit to play."[25]

To be sure, Gehrig's streak, even at 1,808 games, was impressive considering the conditions a ballplayer was forced to endure in the 1920s and 1930s. Aside from the inevitable batting slumps and the assortment of small but nagging aches and pains, ballplayers of Gehrig's day were more vulnerable to serious injury because they didn't wear batting helmets. The career of Mickey Cochrane, the great catcher and player-manager of the Detroit Tigers, came to an abrupt end in 1937 at Yankee Stadium when Bump Hadley hit him with a wild pitch on the left temple, fracturing his skull.[26] Lou himself was beaned severely on at least one occasion (June 29, 1934, in an exhibition game against the Newark Bears) and probably suffered close calls several other times. Gehrig was no stranger to pain. X-rays taken of his hands in 1938 revealed seventeen healed fractures. He had broken every finger of both hands and some of them twice.[27] According to teammate Bill Werber, Lou managed to play through the pain by "trying to catch the ball in the webbing of his glove when the infielders threw it to him." But even then, "if the ball hit him in the palm of his hand the pain must have been excruciating."[28] In addition, the Iron Horse had to endure an exhausting 154-game schedule dominated by sleepless nights in hot, sticky hotel rooms and grueling train rides, some as long as twelve hours if the destination was St. Louis. In the absence of air travel and air conditioning, these conditions eventually took their toll on the players.[29]

One notable critic of Gehrig's quest to reach 2,500 games was Babe Ruth, who, even in retirement, still harbored ill feelings toward his former teammate. "This 'Iron Man' stuff is just baloney," he scoffed. "I think he's making one of the worst mistakes a ballplayer can make. The guy ought to learn to sit on the bench and rest."[30] True to form, Gehrig dismissed the remark, careful to avoid any mention of Ruth's name. Instead, he failed to "see why anyone should belittle [his] record or attack it" as he made it a point to "never belittle anyone else." He also insisted that he would "not play if [his] value to the club is endangered."[31]

Gehrig's streak reached 1,900 games during the 1937 campaign and the Yankees clinched another pennant, finishing thirteen games ahead of second-place Detroit. Gehrig had another great year, hitting .351 with 37 homers and 159 RBIs, while DiMaggio hit .346 and led the American League in runs scored (151), slugging (.673), and home runs (46). Along with Bill Dickey (.332, 29 HR, 133 RBIs), Gehrig and DiMaggio gave the Yankees the most devastating offensive trio in the league, earning for themselves the name "Bronx Bombers."[32] The Yanks defeated the New York Giants once again in the World Series, this time 4 games to 1. Gehrig went 5 for 17 with 1 home run and 3 RBIs for a .294 average, while DiMaggio went 6 for 22 with a homer and 4 RBIs for a .273 average.[33]

It was during the 1930s that Gehrig, unwittingly, began to forge his own legend as an All-American hero. His strong moral code and friendly disposition endeared him to teammates and opponents alike. "The idea that veteran ballplayers didn't treat rookies nicely just wasn't true when it came to Lou," insisted Tommy Henrich. "When I joined the Yankees in 1936 he would help me any way he could."[34] Gehrig respected his teammates as well as his opponents, black or white. When asked how he felt about being compared to Negro Leaguer Walter "Buck" Leonard of the Homestead Grays, who was called the "black Lou Gehrig," the Iron Horse was flattered by the comparison. Lou, who barnstormed against Leonard, said that he "belonged in the major leagues" and that "there's no room in baseball for discrimination if we really believe it's our national pastime and a game for all."[35]

Just as important to Gehrig was his relationship with the fans, especially the young ones. Youngsters flocked to him requesting an autograph. Never would he refuse, even after a tough loss. "Once I saw Lou so upset after we dropped a game that we needed badly," recalled Bill Dickey. "A kid asked him for an autograph and Lou ignored him. He walked a few steps away from the kid, then I heard him mumble to himself and he walked back to give the kid his signature. To be extra considerate, he even chatted with him for a few minutes."[36] Lou also made sure to do his smoking in the dugout tunnel out of the view of young fans so he wouldn't risk promoting a bad habit.[37] His consideration for others was all the more refreshing because it was given with no expectation of personal gain or publicity. Behaving in a gentlemanly fashion was a responsibility he accepted wholeheartedly as the price for being a big league ballplayer. That personal sense of responsibility sometimes made it extremely difficult for Lou to ask for a raise in salary, although his consistently outstanding performance warranted it.

Having helped the Yankees to six pennants and five world championships over the course of a thirteen-year career—including back-to-back Series titles in 1936 and 1937—Gehrig mustered the courage to ask for a $10,000 increase in salary for the 1938 season. "This is going to be my fourteenth season as a regular, and it seems to me that what I ask is not out of reason," he allegedly told Colonel Ruppert. At the same time, Lou didn't believe that a contract dispute should "be aired in public" and that the Yankee owner had the ultimate say on "inviting [him] back."[38] Thus, after a brief holdout, the Iron Horse signed for $39,000, a career high for him.[39]

DiMaggio was not as receptive to the Yankees' offer of $25,000, insisting that his performance commanded a $45,000 salary.[40] Such an outrageous demand for a third-year player earned him harsh criticism from the front office. Shocked by DiMaggio's arrogance, Ed Barrow pointed out that "not even Gehrig made that much money and he's the best player on the team."

"What do you have to say to that?" added the Yankee general manager.

"It's too bad that Gehrig is so underpaid," replied the brash young outfielder.[41]

DiMaggio refused to go to spring training, holding out until three days into the 1938 campaign. Considering the $1,850 the Yankees fined him for the 11 days it took Joe D to get into shape, he ended up signing for $23,150 that season.[42] Interestingly, DiMaggio's stubbornness was, according to the New York sportswriters, part of his appeal. Jack Miley of the *Daily News* pointed out that while Gehrig "towed the line" in contract negotiations, DiMaggio's tendency to "buck the system" was part of his magnetism. "Lou is a helluva good ballplayer, but he lacks color," wrote Miley. "You can't smear 'color' on with a brush. When it comes to personal magnetism, you've either got it or you don't. DiMaggio, like Ruth, has it; but not Gehrig."[43]

Eleanor disagreed. She hired publicist Christy Walsh to promote her husband, just as he had done for Babe Ruth years before.[44] Walsh tried to change Gehrig's bland public image by writing syndicated newspaper articles under Lou's name and arranging endorsements of everything from baseball equipment to breakfast cereals.[45] He even tried to pave the way for a post-baseball career in the movies. Walsh had Lou pose for several beefcake photographs as Tarzan, in an attempt to find a replacement for the Olympic gold-medal swimmer, Johnny Weissmuller, who had retired from the movie role. But the producers balked at the idea when they saw Lou in leopard skins, believing that his broad buttocks and thick legs did not fit the aesthetic image they wanted.[46] Even Weissmuller himself had to laugh when he learned of the scheme. "I guess they'll be making me a ballplayer next," he chortled. "I'll need some first baseman lessons."[47]

Walsh was a bit more successful in exploiting Gehrig's quiet masculinity for a Hollywood western titled *Rawhide*. Gehrig, who in real life was a big fan of B westerns, plays himself in the film, which was produced by Sol Lesser. The plot calls for him to hold out for a better contract by going West to live on a ranch with his sister, Peggy, played by Evalyn Knapp. When Gehrig arrives there he is pressured to surrender his land by a band of crooks. True to his "good guy" image, Lou teams up with a singing lawyer, Larry Kimball, played by Smith Ballew. Together they run the outlaws off the range. In the final scene, Gehrig receives a telegram from the Yankees agreeing to his contract terms and happily heads off to spring training.[48]

Gehrig was not very comfortable with the role of a cowboy actor. His stiff-legged stance and overemphatic dialogues overwhelmed an impressive screen presence, which was largely due to his muscular physique. The reviewers savaged his performance. "As an actor, he's a good first baseman," concluded the *New York Daily News*. "He ought to let it go at that!" The *Daily Mirror* was less complimentary. "Gehrig is no mushy actor . . . in fact, he's no actor at all!"[49] Unfazed by the criticism, Lou gladly returned to baseball and put any notion of an acting career behind him.

The Iron Horse got off to a slow start in 1938. His batting average hovered around the .250 mark through mid-season and McCarthy decided to drop him in the order to fifth, behind DiMaggio in the clean-up slot. Still, Gehrig was unfaltering in the field as he continued to extend his consecutive game streak. On the morning of May 31, with the Boston Red Sox in town to face the Yanks, Eleanor, who worried that the streak was taking its toll on Lou, suggested that he stay at home. "Just skip the game," she told him. "Stop at 1,999, people will remember the streak better at that figure."

Appalled by the suggestion, Lou exploded. "You can't be serious! They've got a little ceremony prepared for me at the Stadium today. I just can't walk out on them. Colonel Ruppert would never forgive me if I didn't show up."[50]

Once she realized how much she had hurt Lou, Eleanor apologized. "Lou, you're smarter than all the rest of us," she said, assuaging his feelings. "You just go on being yourself because that's the guy people love."[51]

Gehrig did, indeed, play in his 2,000th game that day, a 12–5 rout of the Red Sox, and was rewarded with a floral horseshoe afterwards.[52] But he continued to struggle at the plate, and the longer he struggled the harder he worked.

By early August, he had improved his average to the .270 mark, but he was still frustrated with himself. "What the hell, I've tried everything," he despaired to his close friend Bill Dickey. "With all the changes I've made in my batting stance I'm still not hitting the ball. I'm going back to my old way. I certainly can't do any worse."[53] Gehrig forced himself out of the slump, hitting at a .400 clip during the last two months of the season as the Yankees coasted to a third straight pennant. He finished the year with a .295 average (the lowest since his rookie year), 29 home runs (the lowest since 1928), and 114 RBIs (the lowest since 1926).[54] It was the last productive season of his career.

The Yankees clinched the World Series in four straight games, defeating the Chicago Cubs by scores of 3–1, 6–3, 5–2, and 8–3. Lou could only manage 4 base hits in 14 at-bats and didn't knock in a single run. Instead, DiMaggio, Dickey, and second baseman Joe Gordon carried the team to their third straight world championship.[55]

During the Yankees' victory celebration at the Commodore Hotel, Lou, who didn't drink much at all, became inebriated. It was so out of character for him that a teammate approached Eleanor and suggested, "You'd better look after Lou. He's drinking triples, and he's really bombed."[56]

Something was terribly wrong. The Iron Horse knew it, too.

## NOTES

1. Robinson, *Iron Horse*, 212.
2. Tommy Henrich quoted in Bak, *American Classic*, 139.
3. Gallagher and LaConte, *Yankee Encyclopedia*, 386.
4. Dickey quoted in Allen, *Where Have You Gone?* 62–63.
5. Richard Ben Cramer, *Joe DiMaggio: The Hero's Life* (New York: Simon & Schuster, 2000), 50–52.
6. Ibid., 69–71.
7. Allen, *Where Have You Gone?* 15.
8. Dan Daniel quoted in ibid., 16.
9. Don Hallman, "DiMag Hits 3, Yanks Win, 14–5," *New York Daily News*, May 4, 1936.
10. Babe Ruth quoted in Jimmy Powers, "Babe Picks Successor," *New York Daily News*, August 29, 1937.
11. George Selkirk quoted in Allen, *Where Have You Gone?* 17.
12. Lefty Gomez quoted in Bak, *American Classic*, 124.
13. Bak, *American Classic*, 126. DiMaggio was forever grateful to Gehrig for coming to his defense. "When you're a rookie," he said, "you never forget things like that."
14. Ray Robinson, "Lou Gehrig: Columbia Legend and American Hero," *Columbia University Alumni Magazine*, Fall, 2001, 4.
15. Gehrig to Quentin Reynolds quoted in *Sport Magazine's All-Time All Stars*, ed. Tom Murray (New York: Sport Magazine, 1965), 68.
16. Gallagher and LaConte, *Yankee Encyclopedia*, 387.
17. Gehrig quoted in *New York World Telegram*, February 11, 1937.
18. Gallico, *Pride of Yankees*, 123–124.
19. Ibid., 120; and Gehrig and Durso, *My Luke and I*, 4.
20. Robinson, *Iron Horse*, 211.
21. Gallico, *Pride of the Yankees*, 118–119.
22. See Milton Richman, "Mrs. Gehrig Likes to Talk about Lou," *New York Daily News*, August 8, 1973; and Bak, *American Classic*, 138–139.
23. Dan Daniel, "Doctors Say Tiny Ticker Gives Lou Durability," *New York World Telegram*, September 30, 1936.
24. Gehrig quoted in *New York World Telegram*, February 11, 1937.
25. Ibid.
26. Charlie Bevis, *Mickey Cochrane: The Life of a Baseball Hall of Fame Catcher* (Jefferson, NC: McFarland, 1998), 191.
27. Gallico, *Pride of the Yankees*, 134–135.
28. Bill Werber quoted in ESPN Classics, *Sports Century: Lou Gehrig*.
29. Bob Dolgan, "Iron Man Lou Gehrig Played in the Shadow of Babe Ruth," *Baseball Digest*, November 1995, 78.

30. Babe Ruth quoted in Bak, *American Classic*, 141.
31. Gehrig quoted in Robinson, *Iron Horse*, 224.
32. Gallagher and LaConte, *Yankee Encyclopedia*, 387.
33. Wolff, *Baseball Encyclopedia*, 2662.
34. Tommy Henrich quoted in Brett Topel, "Yankee Teammates Recall the Greatness of Lou Gehrig," *Baseball Digest*, July 1995, 28.
35. Gehrig quoted in Bak, *American Classic*, 143.
36. Gallico, *Pride of the Yankees*, 7–8.
37. Bak, *American Classic*, 139.
38. Gehrig quoted in *New York World Telegram*, February 11, 1938.
39. Bak, *American Classic*, 135.
40. Ibid.
41. Allen, *Where Have You Gone?* 34–35.
42. Tofel, *Legend in the Making*, 38.
43. Jack Miley quoted in Cramer, *DiMaggio: Hero's Life*, 110.
44. Creamer, *Babe*, 208–209.
45. Graham, *Quiet Hero*, 246–247.
46. Robinson, *Iron Horse*, 217.
47. Weissmuller quoted in ibid.
48. Hal Erickson, *Baseball in the Movies: A Comprehensive Reference, 1915–1991* (Jefferson, NC: McFarland, 1992), 359.
49. For reviews of *Rawhide* see Bak, *American Classic*, 133.
50. Gehrig quoted in Robinson, *Iron Horse*, 234. According to Paul Gallico, publicist Christy Walsh made the suggestion to end the streak at 1,999 games. He believed that the action would give Gehrig's otherwise bland personality some "color." "If I have to do nutty things like that to have 'color,' " Lou snapped, "I don't want to have any!" See Gallico, *Pride of Yankees*, 131–132.
51. Eleanor Gehrig quoted in Gallico, *Pride of the Yankees*, 132.
52. Bak, *American Classic*, 145.
53. Lou Gehrig quoted in ibid.
54. Honig, *Power Hitters*, 37. The final home run of Gehrig's career came on September 27, 1938, at Yankee Stadium off of Washington's Dutch Leonard.
55. Wolff, *Baseball Encyclopedia*, 2663.
56. Gehrig and Durso, *My Luke and I*, 5.

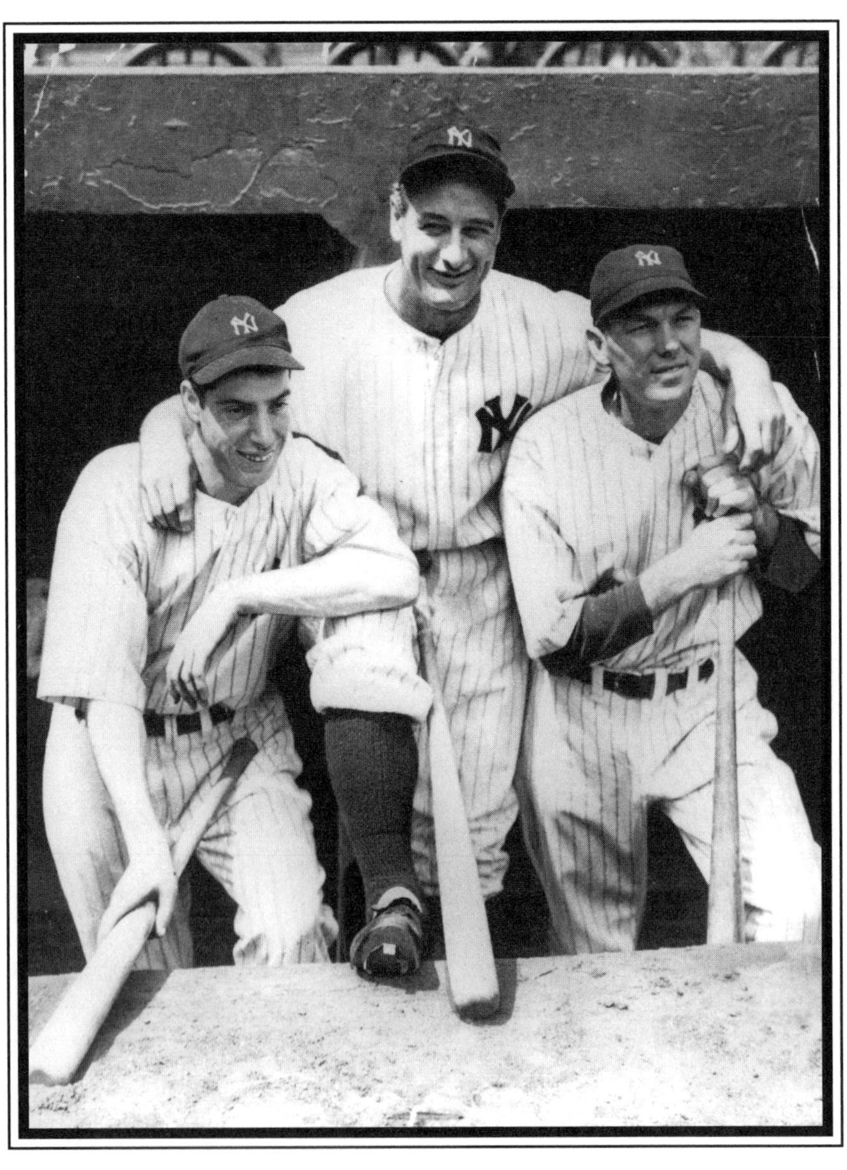

In 1939, Lou Gehrig poses with his best friend and roommate, Bill Dickey (*right*), and Joe DiMaggio (*left*), the rising young star of the Yankees. *National Baseball Hall of Fame Library, Cooperstown, N.Y.*

7

# Quiet Courage, 1939–1941

The winter of 1938–39 was a troubling time for Lou Gehrig. In previous years he was able to enjoy his time away from the game indulging in two of his favorite hobbies: fishing on Long Island Sound and ice-skating on the frozen lakes of Westchester. But news of Nazi Germany's war preparations disturbed him.

Because of his German extraction and the discrimination he experienced as a child during World War I, Gehrig felt very keenly the threat of a German-instigated world war. He considered those German-Americans who supported Hitler's cause "a disgrace," especially since they had immigrated to the United States to enjoy the privileges of democratic citizenship. "As war got closer and closer, you couldn't get him to talk about anything but the defense of democracy," recalled close friend and teammate Bill Dickey. "Once he became so agitated that he told me, 'I'd like to smack some of those skulls a lot harder than I ever hit a baseball.' "[1] Almost as disturbing for Lou was the $3,000 salary cut he agreed to take because of his "off year" in 1938. Instead of complaining about his $36,000 contract, he simply vowed to "work even harder" to regain his form.[2] But even that proved to be difficult.

Some days he didn't feel well. On others, he would go ice-skating with Eleanor and find himself tripping over his skates or even falling, something he almost never did. Concerned, Lou went to see a specialist who dismissed the problem as an upset gall bladder and put him on a special diet.[3]

Although the problem persisted, the Iron Horse continued to believe that it was nothing more than the usual stiffening experienced by most aging veterans and that he could work himself back into shape. He reported to spring training on February 26, along with the Yankee pitchers and catchers, even though position players were not scheduled to report until March 6.[4] Awakening early in the morning, Gehrig would run on his own and then force himself through the regular workout with the team. Afterwards, he spent an hour doing various stretching exercises. But the harder he worked the worse he seemed to play.[5] During one batting practice session, Joe DiMaggio was shocked to see Gehrig miss nineteen swings in a row. "They were all fastballs," he observed, "the kind of pitches that Lou would normally hit into the next county. You could see his timing was way off. He also had trouble catching balls at first base. Sometimes he didn't move his hands fast enough to protect himself."[6]

By mid-March, after playing in ten exhibition games, Lou was barely hitting over .100 with no extra-base hits. He also labored on the base paths. In a game against the Philadelphia Phillies at Clearwater, Florida, Tommy Henrich noted that Lou "looked like he was trying to run uphill at a forty-five degree angle." He was "running as hard as he could, and not getting anywhere."[7] McCarthy, concerned about Gehrig's performance, made plans to use Henrich or Babe Dahlgren as back-ups.[8] "Frankly, I don't know about him," the Yankee manager told Joe Williams of the *New York World Telegram*. "He has lost his speed, and at his age this is something he will never get back. What we don't know is whether he has lost his wrist action at the plate. If he has lost that, then we have no alternative but to get somebody else to play first base."[9]

Speculation among the sportswriters ran the gamut from those who believed that Gehrig's consecutive game streak had finally caught up with him, to those who felt his problems were due to age. Regardless of their perspective, the writers realized that they were witnessing the end of a remarkable career. Initially, Lou, who was never a great interview, tried to dispel any concern about his failing health by telling the scribes, "I've been worried about my hits since 1925. You fellows should know that I never hit in spring training. I just have to work harder than ever."[10] But as Lou continued to labor it became extremely difficult for him to deal with the press. Near the end of spring training, Vincent Flaherty of the Orlando, Florida, *Morning Sentinel* approached Gehrig and questioned him about his future with the team. Enraged by the inquiry, Lou demanded that he be "left alone." The next day, Flaherty, who took exception to the New York sportswriters' nostalgic—if not sentimental—coverage of Gehrig, wrote a vengeful column. Condemning the "maudlin slobbering" of the Big Apples' scribes, Flaherty claimed that he was "not in St. Petersburg to praise Gehrig," but rather to "bury the bloke." In an especially damning article Flaherty wrote, "When Gehrig goes, I'll be sitting in on the requiem of a selfish, surly tightwad, who milked the game of all he could and who walked through his career filled with the self-sufficient philosophy that the world owed him everything."[11] The characterization was so atypical of Gehrig and so unfair that the other writers turned on Flaherty. Lou was determined to have revenge on the playing field.

When the Yanks broke camp to head north, they stopped at Norfolk, Virginia, to play the Brooklyn Dodgers in a four-game series. Gehrig showed signs of his old self by collecting four hits, two of which were home runs. McCarthy, however, was not impressed, observing that both round trippers were "hit over a short right field fence."[12] Nevertheless, the four hits enabled Lou to raise his spring training average to .215 with 26 hits and 21 RBIs in 121 at-bats, and lessen Yankee concerns about the eight errors he committed at first base during the short docket of preseason games.[13] McCarthy, aware that he could rely on the hitting of DiMaggio, Henrich, Dickey, Keller, Gordon, and Crosetti to carry his team, decided to stick with Gehrig at first base.

The Yankees opened the 1939 season on April 20 against the Boston Red Sox. Lou, who started his 2,123rd straight game, went hitless. In his first at-bat, he stranded two runners, lining out to right fielder Ted Williams. "He hit a humpbacked line drive to me his first time up," remembered Williams, who was in his rookie year. "I seem to recall that he swung down on the ball a bit, but he still had amazing power."[14] In the fifth inning, Gehrig came to bat again with Jake Powell on third and one out. Lefty Grove, who was in the twilight of his own Hall of Fame career, had intentionally walked DiMaggio to get to Gehrig. While the act insulted Lou deeply since Grove had always treated him with respect as a hitter, it worked for the Red Sox as Gehrig hit into a double play. Still, the Yankees managed to win the opener and defeated the Red Sox again the following day to sweep the two-game series. Lou managed to collect his first hit of the season but also committed a fielding error on a routine ground ball in the 6–3 Yankee win.[15]

Gehrig went hitless in the next three games, as the Yanks dropped two against the Washington Senators before defeating the Philadelphia Athletics 2–1 at Yankee Stadium on April 24.[16] "I think there's something wrong with him," wrote James Kahn of the *New York Graphic*:

> I mean something physically wrong. . . . I don't know what it is, but I'm satisfied that it goes far beyond his ball playing. I have seen ballplayers "go" overnight. But they were simply washed up as ballplayers. It's something deeper in this case, though. I have watched him very closely and this is what I have seen: I have seen him time a ball perfectly, swing on it as hard as he can, meet it squarely—and drive a soft, looping fly over the infield. In other words, for

> some reason that I do not know, his old power isn't there. He is meeting the ball, time after time, and it isn't going anywhere."[17]

Bill Dickey also began to notice that his roommate was suffering from something more than the declining skills of an aging veteran.

> Lou had always been very even-tempered, easy and pleasant, but now he'd sit in the room and say nothing at all for a long time. When I'd try to cheer him up and tell him I thought he was coming around at last, he would hardly even answer me. I was beginning to realize that there was something the matter with him. Something that had nothing to do with him getting older. . . . Then one day something happened in the room that convinced me. He started to take a little step forward to get something and the foot he moved forward to start the step just didn't move right. Instead of swinging right out, it just moved a few inches in a faltering kind of way and it threw Lou off balance, and he stumbled to the floor. He looked up with a shocked and embarrassed expression. A few days later the same thing happened in the clubhouse. He took a real bad fall as he started to undress. Nobody wanted to humiliate him by going to his aid and he dragged himself off the floor, looking sort of dazed, as if someone struck him down from behind.[18]

On April 25, the Yankees defeated the A's again, 8–4, and Lou collected 2 hits, but his teammates were now questioning the wisdom of his playing all the consecutive games without a rest. So were the sportswriters, who became increasingly critical of the Iron Horse's play. Paul Gallico of the *New York Daily News* admitted that those stories "saddened" many of the writers who had "grown to love Lou." At the same time, however, the scribes "owed a loyalty to their papers and to the people who read them to write what they see."[19] Gehrig understood that fact, publicly stating that he "expected a square deal" from the writers. "I don't expect anybody to write anything but his honest reaction to what he sees," he told Dan Daniel of the *New York World Telegram.*[20] At the same time, Lou took complete responsibility for his poor play, attributing his difficulties to a "lazy off season," during which he "should have been jogging every day."[21]

After a few rainouts, the Yanks resumed play on April 29, losing to Washington, 3–1. Lou, playing in his 2,129th straight game, collected a single off the Senators' Ken Chase; it would be the final hit of his career.[22] Gehrig was hitting just .143 and was sluggish in the field. Teammates began to express their concern about his slow reflexes and whether he was able to get out of the way of a high, hard fastball. But McCarthy realized that he couldn't bench Lou for just a game or two when he was riding an unbroken string of games and he had too much respect for his first baseman to pull him from the line-up.[23] As far as the Yankee manager was concerned, Lou would have to bench himself.

On Sunday, April 30, Lou reported to Yankee Stadium early to take some extra batting practice. It didn't matter—he went hitless in the 3–2 loss to Washington.[24] Worse, Lou felt he was being patronized by his teammates. In the ninth inning, when he fielded a routine ground ball, pitcher Johnny Murphy shot off the mound to cover first base on what should have been an easy, unassisted play. When Gehrig returned to the bench his teammates were congratulating him for "a great play."

"For heaven's sake," the bewildered slugger thought to himself, "has it reached that stage?"[25]

After the game, in the clubhouse, some of the Yankees openly questioned whether the team could win with Gehrig in the line-up. Although Lou heard the remarks, he chose to ignore them.[26]

"They don't think I can do it anymore," he told Eleanor when he returned home that evening. "Maybe I can, maybe I can't. But they're talking about it now. They're even writing about it. And when they're not talking, I can almost feel what they're thinking. Then, I wish to God that they would talk—you know, say anything instead of sitting there looking at me."

"You've done it for thirteen years without a day off," she replied. "All that matters is if you still get satisfaction out of playing."

"How can I get satisfaction? I'm not giving them the same thing, so I'm not getting the same thing. You think they're hurting me. But I'm hurting *them*, that's the difference."

There was an awkward silence. Neither husband nor wife knew what to say. Finally, Eleanor, choosing her words carefully, reminded Lou, "You've always said you would step down as soon as you felt you could no longer help the team. Maybe that time's come."[27]

Lou spent the next day wrestling with the decision as he traveled with the team to Detroit for a three-game series against the Tigers. Frustrated and feeling guilty about his poor performance, Gehrig, on the morning of May 2, called on McCarthy at his room at the Book-Cadillac Hotel. "Nobody has to tell me how bad I've been playing and how much of a drawback I've been to the club," began Lou, choking back his emotions. "I've been thinking ever since the season opened when I couldn't start as I hoped I would, that the time has come for me to quit for the good of the team."

"You don't have to quit," interrupted McCarthy, almost apologetically. "Take a rest for a week or so, and maybe you'll feel all right again."

It was wishful thinking. "I don't know," said Lou. "I just can't figure out what's the matter with me. I just know I can't go on this way."

Gehrig proceeded to describe the routine play he made against the Senators earlier in the week and how his teammates applauded his effort. "I knew then that it was time to get out."

After listening attentively, McCarthy agreed with the decision. "All right, Lou," he said. "But any time you want to get back in there, it's your position. I'll put Dahlgren in at first today."[28]

On the way back to his room, the Iron Horse was greeted by Wally Pipp, the man he replaced at first base thirteen years earlier. Pipp, who lived in Grand Rapids, Michigan, had come to visit his old team. After some small talk, Gehrig told Pipp that he wasn't feeling well and that he probably wouldn't be playing that afternoon.[29] Whether the remark didn't register with Pipp, or he simply dismissed it, will never be known. But the magnitude of the decision would not be lost on the fans.

Before that afternoon's game at Tiger Stadium, Gehrig, with line-up card in hand, walked stiffly out to the umpires gathered at home plate. He would not be playing for the first time in thirteen years. Instead, the name "Dahlgren" was inserted into the line-up at first base. The Detroit fans, suddenly realizing that they were witnessing a historic moment, took to their feet for a two-minute ovation in appreciation of the Iron Horse. Blinking back tears, the Yankee slugger acknowledged the crowd with a tip of his hat and retreated to the visitors' dugout. There, he found a seat on the bench, buried his head in his hands, and wept. It was an awkward moment for his teammates, who were unsure of how to handle the situation. Finally, Lefty Gomez broke the silence. "Hey, Lou!" he called out. "It took fifteen years to get you out of the game. Sometimes I'm out in fifteen minutes."[30] The wisecrack made Gehrig laugh and eased the tension on the Yankee bench.

During the game a photographer asked Lou to pose as if he were cheering on his 27-year-old successor, Babe Dahlgren. Gehrig politely declined, saying that he planned to return to the line-up soon.[31] Although New York went on to rout the Tigers 22–2, "there was little to celebrate" according to left-fielder George Selkirk. "After Lou's decision, we knew it would never be the same."[32]

The next morning as he sat in his hotel room contemplating the future, Lou wrote to Eleanor about his decision to bench himself:

> It was inevitable, although I dreaded the day and my thoughts were with you constantly. How would this affect you and I? That was the big question and the most important thought underlying everything. I broke just before the game because of thoughts of you. . . .

> As for me, the road may come to a dead end here, but why should it? Seems like our backs are to the wall now, but there usually comes a way out—where and what, I know not, but who can tell that it might not lead right out to some greater things?[33]

With Gehrig out of the line-up, the Yankees soon rediscovered their winning ways. After the May 2nd drubbing of the Tigers, they won twenty-eight of their next thirty-two games. Lou remained in uniform, although delivering the line-up card would be his sole duty for the remainder of the season. Often, he could be found sitting in the dugout in tears. As painful as the sight might have been, McCarthy was relieved by Gehrig's decision to bench himself. "It's just as well he made up his mind to get out," he admitted. "I never wanted to hear people shout at him, 'Ya big bum, ya' if Lou made an out or messed up a ball. He's been too grand a fellow, too big a figure in baseball for that sort of thing."[34]

As the spring wore on there was a noticeable decline in Gehrig's appearance. He was not only losing weight, but his hair was graying at the temples and his hands lost so much dexterity that he couldn't deal the cards when he played bridge. Eleanor began to fear that he had a brain tumor and scheduled an appointment for him at the famed Mayo Clinic in Rochester, Minnesota.[35]

On June 12, a day before he was to leave for the clinic, Lou played in his very last game. It was an exhibition contest against the Yankees' top farm club, the Kansas City Blues. The Blues featured a formidable line-up of future big leaguers in Phil Rizzuto, Jerry Priddy, Clyde McCullough, and Vince DiMaggio. Although Gehrig was not scheduled to play, he told McCarthy that he felt an obligation to the 23,864 fans who had come out to the game to make an appearance. The Yankee manager agreed to let him play. Hitting eighth, Lou grounded out to second baseman Jerry Priddy in his only time up. Still, the Kansas City fans gave him a standing ovation. Gehrig left the game after the third inning to return to the hotel to get a good rest for the flight to Rochester the next morning.[36]

On June 13, Gehrig entered the Mayo Clinic for a thorough examination. The Yankees tried to downplay the trip by arranging a visit with Julie Wera—a teammate on the 1927 Yankees and a Rochester resident—and a speaking engagement with the city's American Legion Baseball team.[37]

Gehrig was assigned to Dr. Henry Woltman, head of the neurology department, but Dr. Harold Habien, Mayo's chief diagnostician was the first to meet with him. After observing Lou's "shuffling gait, his handshake, and his overall expression," Habien knew immediately that the Yankee slugger was suffering from amyotrophic lateral sclerosis (ALS), the same disease that had claimed the life of Habien's own mother.[38] The next five days of tests proved Habien's instincts correct. On Monday, June 19, Lou's thirty-sixth birthday, Woltman broke the bad news to him.[39]

Woltman explained that ALS is a rare neurological disorder that affects the spinal cord and lower brainstem. Victims experience a progressive degeneration of the nerve cells in these areas that stimulate movement in the arms, legs, trunk, neck, and head. As the nerve cells harden, there is a weakening of the muscles, initially in the arms or legs. Paralysis follows with the loss of the ability to walk, to use arms or hands, to swallow, and, ultimately, to even breathe. Typically symptoms appear in middle- to late-adulthood and death usually follows within two to five years. Throughout the disease, the victim has complete control of his mental faculties. There is no known cause for ALS, nor is there any treatment.[40]

That evening Lou wrote to Eleanor, marginalizing the severity of the disease:

> *Mornin' Sweet:*
>
> *Really, I don't know how to start and I'm not much at breaking news gently. But am going to write it as there is no use in keeping you in suspense. I'll tell it all, just as it is.*
>
> *As for breaking this news to the papers, I thought and the doctors approved, that they write a medical report and then a laymen's* [sic] *interpretation underneath and I would tell the paper men here that I felt it was my duty to my employers that they have firsthand information and that I felt sure they would give it to the newspapermen. That seemed the most logical way to all of us here and I felt it was such vital news that it wouldn't be fair to have Joe [McCarthy] and Ed [Barrow] read about it in the papers.*
>
> *However, don't be too alarmed or sympathetic, for the most important thing for me is no fatigue and no strain or major worries. The bad news is "amyotrophic lateral sclerosis." There isn't any cure, the best they can hope is to check it at the point it is now and there is a 50-50 chance for that.*
>
> *There are very few of these cases. It is probably caused by some germ. However, my first question was transmission. No danger whatever. Never heard of transmitting it to mates. If there were (and I made them doubly assure me) you certainly would never have been allowed within 100 feet of me.*
>
> *I may need a cane in ten or fifteen years. Playing is out of the question and Paul suggests a coaching job or job in the office or writing. I made him honestly assure me that it will not affect me mentally.*
>
> *They seem to think I'll get along all right if I can reconcile myself to*

*this condition, which I have done but only after they assured me there is no danger of transmission and that I will not become mentally unbalanced and thereby become a burden on your hands for life.*

*I adore you, sweetheart.*[41]

Because of his deep and abiding love for Eleanor, Lou tried to protect her from the painful reality that he had just two years to live. But unbeknownst to him, Dr. Charles Mayo had already telephoned to inform her of the diagnosis. "It hit me amidships," she would recall years later. "It took me two days to get the crying out of my system for my new role and the new 'front' that went with it."[42]

When Lou flew back to New York on June 21, Eleanor was there to meet him at Newark Airport in their Packard, and the "conspiracy of silence" began. There would be no brooding, no false hopes, just living from day to day and enjoying life at the present moment.[43] About 12:30 P.M., the Gehrigs arrived at Yankee Stadium where they met with McCarthy and Barrow to inform them of the Mayo's verdict. Ten minutes later, the Yankee clubhouse was opened to the sportswriters.

"Gentlemen," began Barrow, "we have bad news. Lou Gehrig has infantile paralysis. The technical word for his illness is chronic poliomyelitis. He has been given a chart of exercises and a list of doctors by the Mayo Clinic. Lou will be given treatment throughout the summer, as the list covers all cities the Yankees will visit. The report recommends that Lou abandon any hope of continuing as an active player."

Barrow went on to say that the Iron Horse would be retained on the Yankee roster as an active player and paid his full salary of $36,000 for the remainder of the season, after which he would be given his unconditional release.[44] The next day newspapers across the nation carried the sad news, along with the following statement released by the Mayo Clinic: "Mr. Lou Gehrig is suffering from amyotrophic lateral sclerosis . . . and will be unable to continue his active participation as a baseball player, inasmuch as it is advisable that he conserve his muscular energy."[45]

Plans for a "Lou Gehrig Appreciation Day" were made. The event was to be held between games of a July 4 double-header against the Washington Senators. On that day, 61,808 fans packed Yankee Stadium to show their appreciation for the Iron Horse.[46] Lou appreciated the gesture but was "scared silly," admitting that he'd rather strike out in the ninth with the score tied, two down, and the bases loaded than walk out there before all those people."[47] Although the Bronx Bombers dropped the first game, 3–2, the spirits of the crowd were high as Sid Mercer, master of ceremonies, began to announce the names of Lou's former teammates who had come to honor him—Wally Pipp, Everett Scott, Wally Schang, and Babe Ruth, among others. These former Yankees joined the Senators along the first base side of the infield between home plate and the pitcher's mound. The current Yankee players formed a line along the third base side. After the introductions, Lou stepped out onto the field. Slowly and stiffly, he made his way to home plate, conscious of his physical and emotional vulnerability. McCarthy warned several players to keep their eyes peeled on Lou, who appeared ready to collapse at any moment.[48]

General Manager Ed Barrow stepped to the microphone and announced that Gehrig's uniform number 4 would be retired, the first time in baseball history that such an honor was bestowed. Next came the presentation of gifts—a silver tea service from the Yankees, a fruit bowl from the rival New York Giants, a fishing rod and tackle from the Yankee stadium employees, and a tobacco stand from the baseball writers. But the gift that meant the most was presented by McCarthy on behalf of the team. It was a silver trophy mounted on a wooden box in the shape of home plate and inscribed with a poem written by John Kieran of the *New York Times*.[49] In it, Kieran describes the "wars" that were fought as a team throughout the years, and how Gehrig was a true leader, both on and off the field, "for every human test."

When McCarthy presented his beleaguered first baseman with the trophy he confessed that it was "a sad day" when Lou told him he was quitting as a ballplayer because he believed himself to be "a hindrance to the team." "My God, man, you were never that," said the Yankee manager, choking back his emotions.[50]

Gehrig, noticeably moved by the words, accepted the trophy, which he gently placed on the ground in front of him. When McCarthy tried to guide him to the cluster of microphones so he could speak to the crowd, Lou, overcome with emotion, gestured to Mercer to express his appreciation for him. But the crowd began to cheer, "We want Gehrig!" Brushing away tears, Lou shuffled to the microphone, aided by McCarthy. Although he had jotted down some brief remarks the previous evening, the paper remained folded inside his back pocket.[51] Trying hard to collect himself, Lou bowed his head and began to speak:

> Fans, for the past two weeks you have been reading about the bad break I got. Yet today I consider myself the luckiest man on the face of the earth. I have been in ballparks for seventeen years and have never received anything but kindness and encouragement from you fans.

> Look at these grand men. Which of you wouldn't consider it the highlight of his career just to associate with them for even one day? Sure, I'm lucky. Who wouldn't consider it an honor to have known Jacob Ruppert? Also, the builder of baseball's greatest empire, Ed Barrow? To have spent six years with that wonderful little fellow, Miller Huggins? Then to have spent the next nine years with that outstanding leader, that smart student of psychology, the best manager in baseball today, Joe McCarthy? Sure I'm lucky.
>
> When the New York Giants, a team you would give your right arm to beat, and vice versa, sends you a gift—that's something. When everybody down to the groundskeepers and those boys in white coats remember you with trophies—that's something. When you have a wonderful mother-in-law who takes sides with you in squabbles with her own daughter—that's something. When you have a father and a mother who work all their lives so you can have an education and build your body—it's blessing. When you have a wife who has been a tower of strength and shown more courage than you dreamed existed—that's the finest I know.
>
> So I close in saying that I may have had a tough break, but I have an awful lot to live for.

Lou began to take a step back, then quickly leaned toward the microphone and added, "Thank you."[52]

Gehrig's remarks, though just two minutes in length, touched everyone that day. Not only had the words came straight from his heart, but the humble manner in which he delivered them was just as moving. As much as he tried, Lou could not hold back the tears on this bittersweet occasion. On one hand, he was mourning for what he had lost and knew he would never again be able to reclaim. On the other, his tears were the only way he could show how deeply he was moved by all the love and support he had received from others, not just for seventeen years with the Yankees, but for his entire life. The Gehrig legend began with that farewell address, a speech that was later called the "Gettysburg Address of Baseball."[53]

Babe Ruth was so moved that he walked over to Lou, impulsively threw his arm around his former teammate, and whispered something in his ear—the first words the two men had shared in years.[54] Eleanor, impressed by her husband's composure and his ability to recall the speech by heart, was overwhelmed by the experience. "Lou cried, I cried and 61,000 people cried with us," she recalled many years later.[55] Shirley Povich of the *Washington Post*, who witnessed the scene from the press box, waxed more eloquently. "Today I saw strong men weep, expressionless umpires swallow hard, and emotion pump the hearts and glaze the eyes of 61,000 baseball fans in Yankee Stadium as hard-boiled newspaper photographers clicked their cameras with fingers that trembled."[56]

The National Baseball Hall of Fame, which inducted its charter class at Cooperstown, New York, that summer, waived the five-year waiting period and elected Gehrig to its ranks later that year.[57] In addition to retiring Lou's uniform number, the Yankees also sealed his locker and erected a monument in his name in deep centerfield.[58] Gehrig had achieved baseball immortality.

Lou spent the summer living vicariously through his teammates. As Yankee captain, he continued to deliver the line-up card to home plate before each game. Afterwards, he sat in the dugout and watched the game. Sometimes he was astonished to learn just how much he enjoyed watching the contest. "You'd be surprised how different a slant you get on a ball game when you see it from the bench," he admitted to a sportswriter. "I've been playing all these years trying to take care of my own position. Now, for the first time, I am looking at a complete game."[59] Lou also enjoyed the camraderie and the frequent bantering of the players. Often, his Yankee teammates teased him, suggesting that he was "faking" his illness to take an extended vacation and "soak the Yankees for all he could get."[60]

Like the physicians at the Mayo Clinic, McCarthy believed that remaining with the team would be good for Lou because it would take his mind off his illness, giving him the positive mind-set he needed to fight his battle against ALS.[61] In fact, Gehrig was given some hope during a return visit to Mayo in late August when doctors found that his condition had "definitely improved." After he heard the news, Lou chuckled and admitted that he was "feeling right along that [he] was getting better," but that it was "good to get the news direct from headquarters."[62] The positive feedback lifted his spirits so much that he agreed to do an interview that evening with Dwight Merriam of KROC Radio in Rochester, Minnesota. Merriam, sensitive to Gehrig's desire for privacy, limited his questioning to baseball.

The interview offered some rare insight into the Iron Horse's views of a game that was on the verge of some significant changes. When asked, for example, what he thought about night baseball, Gehrig replied, "Well, night baseball is strictly a show and is strictly advantageous to the owner's pocketbook. But as far as being a true exhibition of baseball, I don't think I can say it is." While he admitted that "the men who work in the daytime like to get out at night, and we do all in our power to give them their money's worth," Gehrig insisted that "real baseball should be played in the daytime and in the sunshine." More revealing were his remarks on the possibility of a players' union. Anticipating the decline in player talent, ability, and motivation that accompanied free agency more than three decades later, Gehrig said that a ballplayer's union "would put everybody in the same class," allowing "the inferior ballplayer, the boy who has a tendency to loaf, in the same salary class with the fella who hustles and has great ability and takes advantage of his ability." A player's union "wouldn't work," he concluded, because the truly exceptional talent "would not be rewarded for his abilities."[63]

Gehrig's presence in the Yankee clubhouse and dugout also served to cultivate positive change in the relationship between younger players and the more seasoned veterans. Remembering the difficulty he once had being accepted by the veterans when he was first promoted to the majors, Lou constantly provided rookies like Charlie Keller and Atley Donald with positive reinforcement, but he was careful to offer advice only when asked for it. "The young man, 15 to 20 years ago when I broke in, had to go out and fight his way for a job under many adverse conditions," he recalled. "But the young man today is surrounded with the old timer's advice and experience, which can make him just as good if he's willing to listen."[64]

But there were also those occasions when Lou's presence on the team only served to remind him of his physical deterioration. Once, during a pregame batting practice, George Selkirk picked out a bat and headed for the plate when Lou offered an encouraging word. "Get hot, George. I want to see you hit a couple into the stands today."

Selkirk stopped abruptly, turned in Gehrig's direction and quipped, "What are you telling me what to do for Lou? If you had any guts, you'd get in there and hit a couple yourself!"

The Iron Horse realized that the right fielder was only joking with him, but the remark struck a melancholy note, as he murmured to himself, "I wish to God I could, George."[65]

On another occasion, when the Yankees arrived at a railway station in Washington where they were scheduled to play the Senators, a group of Boy Scouts noticed them and shouted out, "Good luck, Lou!" Gehrig, who was walking with Rud Rennie of the *New York Herald Tribune*, turned, smiled, and waved at the youngsters. Then, turning to Rennie, Gehrig said, "They're wishing me luck . . . and I'm dying."[66]

Lou tried hard to keep things light-hearted around his teammates, not wanting to burden them with his problems. Even though he could no longer contribute with his bat or glove, his presence in the dugout was appreciated and probably inspired the Yanks to capture a record-breaking fourth straight pennant. The 1939 Yankees were among the best teams in baseball history. DiMaggio (.381, 30 HR, 126 RBIs) won the batting championship and the American League's MVP Award. Red Rolfe hit .329 and led the league in runs

(139), hits (213), and doubles (46). Bill Dickey (.302, 24 HR, 105 RBIs), George Selkirk (.306, 21 HR, 101 RBIs), and 22-year-old rookie Charlie Keller (.334, 11 HR, 83 RBIs) also provided offensive punch.

Red Ruffing (21–7, 95 K, 2.94 ERA) was the ace of the staff, having posted his fourth straight season with twenty or more wins. Although Lefty Gomez (12–8, 102 K, 3.41 ERA) saw limited action, being hampered by a sore arm, the pitching was deep enough to carry the team. Atley Donald, a 28-year-old rookie, was an unexpected surprise, posting a13–3 record. Bump Hadley (12–6, 65 K, 2.98 ERA), Monte Pearson (12–5, 76 K, 4.50 ERA), and Steve Sundra (11–1, 27 K, 2.75 ERA) were also dependable starters, and Johnny Murphy led the league in saves with nineteen. Predictably, the Yankees led the league in fielding (.978), pitching (3.31 ERA), and five major batting categories: home runs (166), RBIs (903), slugging average (.451), walks (701), and runs scored (967).

New York clinched the pennant in early September, outdistancing the second-place Red Sox by seventeen games. New York went on to sweep the Cincinnati Reds in the World Series, giving McCarthy the distinction of being the first man in baseball history ever to win four straight championships.[67]

For Gehrig, the Series marked the end of his employment with the Yankees. While general manager Ed Barrow honored his contract and awarded him a full postseason share, he made it clear to Eleanor that "it was time for Lou to get another job" once the season ended.[68] When he learned of the remark, Lou was deeply hurt. He had always considered Barrow a friend and assumed that when his playing days had ended there would be a place for him in the Yankee front office.[69] Now he was at loose ends.

Realizing Gehrig's predicament, Mayor Fiorello La Guardia, on the train ride to Cincinnati for the World Series, asked Lou to join the New York Parole Commission. La Guardia believed that the Iron Horse could be an inspiration to many of the city's wayward youngsters. Lou demurred at first, saying that he knew very little about the law or the responsibilities of the parole commission. But La Guardia refused to take no for an answer. "All you need is common sense," he told Gehrig, "and you have that." After thinking it over, Lou gratefully accepted the appointment, wanting to "give something back" to the city where he was born and raised.[70]

Sworn in for a ten-year term on January 2, 1940, Gehrig was paid $5,700 a year to interview prisoners with undetermined sentences and decide if they were ready for parole. He was assigned 6,000 cases in the first year alone. Because it was a municipal job, city law required that the Gehrigs relocate from their Larchmont home in the suburbs to a residence within the city limits. So the Gehrigs rented a white frame house at 5204 Delafield Avenue in the Riverdale section of the Bronx. Eleanor had the house outfitted with ramps to accommodate her husband, who inevitably would be forced to use a wheelchair.[71]

Each morning Eleanor drove Lou from their new home in Riverdale to his lower Manhattan office. She stayed with her husband as he interviewed the prostitutes, pimps, burglars, and juvenile delinquents who came before him. When Lou lost the use of his hands, Eleanor would nonchalantly light his cigarette, place it in his mouth, and take it out after a puff, while he listened to the stories of the criminals. Some complained that they "got a bad break," aloof to the grave circumstances of their questioner or the irony of their remark.[72] One of the prisoners who came before Lou was a 19-year-old named Rocco Barbella. When the accused rapist arrived for his hearing, Gehrig examined his considerable probation record and remarked, "You've caused your mother a lot of grief, haven't you?"

Barbella responded to the comment with smug indifference, until Lou told him that he had decided to send him to reform school in the hope that he would "straighten himself out."

"Go to hell you bastard!" screamed the juvenile delinquent, who would eventually turn his life around to become Rocky Graziano, the middleweight boxing champion of the world.[73]

In late February, a sportswriter visited Lou at his Manhattan office, curious to know if he missed the annual ritual of spring training. "Sure, I'd like to be going South with the Yankees," replied the Iron Horse. "I had a long stretch in baseball, and I enjoyed every minute of it. Now that's behind me, and I have this work to do."

As the interview unfolded, it became clear that Gehrig was deeply committed to his new work. Pointing to the caseload on his desk, Lou told the writer, "This is important work, too. I have a great responsibility in dealing with the lives of young men, many of them little more than boys. I think that many of them deserve another chance. However, we must also consider the taxpayers and our duties towards them. We don't want anyone in jail who can be good and contribute to society."[74]

The Iron Horse had resigned himself to the fact that his baseball career was over. He might have been bitter—most anyone else would have been given the same circumstances—but he wasn't. Instead, he became immersed, heart and soul, in the work of the parole commission. When he spoke of the Yankees it was always as "we." Lou followed the fortunes of the team closely and never considered himself as anything but a member of it. He frequently attended games. If the Yanks enjoyed a big lead in the late innings, he'd make an early exit to avoid being caught in the rush of the fans. If it was a close game, he'd stay until the end.[75] Once, while visiting with Yankee broadcaster Mel Allen before the game, Lou admitted that he "never listened to the radio broadcasts" during his playing days, but now "all I do is listen. . . . It's the only thing that keeps me going." Allen, deeply moved by the confession, excused himself under the pretense of having to prepare for the broadcast. He barely made it to the runway before he broke down, "bawling like a baby."[76]

Eleanor proved to be Lou's bedrock during these trying times. During the evenings she opened their home to comedians, entertainers, sportswriters, and former teammates, all of whom were sworn to secrecy about the seriousness of Lou's condition. Neither husband nor wife wanted to burden the other with the disturbing knowledge they possessed, so they continued the conspiracy of silence as well as the endless stream of guests in the hope of lifting each other's spirits.

Songwriter Fred Fisher often came to play the piano, even though he was a better lyricist. While Lou enjoyed the recitals, Eleanor once told Fisher, "You sound like a player in a whorehouse."

"I was," he admitted, without missing a beat. "I played at the Everleigh house in Chicago!"[77]

Among the other regulars were John Kieran, a neighbor and sportswriter for the *New York Times*; Pitzy Katz, an old vaudevillian; Ed Barrow and his wife, Fanny; and teammates Bill Dickey, Tommy Henrich, and Frank Crosetti.[78] Dr. Caldwell Esselstyn, another Riverdale neighbor, was designated by the Mayo Clinic to care for Lou. Each morning Esselstyn came by to give the ailing slugger an injection of Vitamin E, considered at the time to provide short-term relief from the debilitating effects of ALS.[79]

As 1940 closed, Lou, who had become significantly weaker, began to work from the house. He dictated correspondence to parolees as well as to other victims of ALS and found pleasure in the company of his small, black-and-white puppy, whom he named "Yankee."[80] He also brought a $1 million lawsuit against sportswriter Jimmy Powers of the *New York Daily News*, who suggested in print that Gehrig's disease spread to his teammates, causing the Yankees' prolonged batting slump and third-place finish that season.[81] The suit was settled out of court for $17,500 after Powers wrote a public apology to Gehrig and the Yankees, admitting that he had "no business getting snarled up in medical controversy" and that "hurting [Gehrig's] feelings was far from my mind."[82] But the incident was deeply hurtful to the Iron Horse.

By spring 1941, Gehrig was bedridden. He had great difficulty controlling his facial muscles and preventing his hands from twitching. Before visitors arrived, Eleanor would fold his arms across his chest to hide his paralyzed fingers. Esselstyn noted that his patient weighed just 120 pounds. Still, Lou refused to surrender to ALS.

"Poor Lou could hardly move his head," observed Jack Kieran shortly after his final visit with Gehrig. "But he said to me, 'This is the crisis, Jack. After this, I'll gradually get better.' I nodded in agreement, ready to cry as I walked home."[83] Former teammates Bill Dickey and Tommy Henrich also called on Gehrig during the final days of his life, astonished at his positive attitude. "I'll never forget as we were walking out the door," recalled Henrich. "Lou called to us and said, 'So long guys. I'm going to beat this thing.' He never lost his positive attitude."[84] Dickey agreed. "It was during the last years of his life that Lou showed his real class," he said. "He must have known the disease had him licked, but he wouldn't admit it. I think he was just trying to keep up a pretense because he didn't want his wife and pals to feel badly. The last time I saw him, just before he died, he went to great lengths to explain that the doctors told him he was reaching a turning point in his sickness and that he would soon improve."[85]

On Monday, June 2, Lou spent the day propped against pillows on his bed, reading and listening to the radio. That night he slipped into a coma and Eleanor called Esselstyn, Mom and Pop Gehrig, and Ed Barrow. Shortly before 10:00 P.M. Lou opened his eyes and saw them all standing beside his bed and told them that they had been "the best pals of [his] lifetime." Then he closed his eyes and slipped away, "the most beautiful expression spreading over his face."[86] The Iron Horse of baseball, just 37 years old, had lost his battle with ALS, sixteen years to the day after he began his 2,130-consecutive-game streak.

News of Gehrig's death stunned the sports world. Yankee manager Joe McCarthy learned the news the next morning when he arrived in Detroit, where his team was scheduled to play the Tigers. Badly shaken, McCarthy sat down in the lobby of the Book-Cadillac Hotel with some of the players who were also stunned by the news. Dickey sat in his room and cried.[87] Tributes poured in from around the country. Mayor La Guardia ordered the city's flags to be flown at half-staff. The New York newspapers carried editorials honoring Gehrig's courage and expressing grief at his untimely death. President Franklin D. Roosevelt sent flowers to Eleanor and more than 1,500 telegrams expressing condolences arrived at the couple's Riverdale home.[88]

On the evening of June 3, Gehrig's body, dressed in a blue, pinstriped business suit, lay in state at Christ Episcopal Church in Riverdale, where the Gehrigs had been parishioners since relocating in the city. An unbroken procession of mourners stood in the rain to pay their last respects to the fallen Yankee.[89] A private funeral service was held the next morning at 10:00 A.M.

with only 100 attendees, including Babe Ruth, Joe McCarthy, Bill Dickey, Ed Barrow, and Baseball Commissioner Judge Kenesaw Mountain Landis.[90] The service lasted just eight minutes in the absence of a eulogy. "There is no need for one," Reverend Gerald Barry told the gathering, "because you all knew him."[91] Bill Dickey echoed the remark afterwards saying, "Lou doesn't need tributes from anyone. His life and the way he lived were tribute enough."[92]

After the service, Gehrig's remains were taken to the Fresh Pond Crematory in Queens, Long Island, where they were cremated in accordance with his wishes. Lou also requested that Eleanor keep the small vase containing his ashes in their house until her death, at which time she, too, would be cremated and their ashes mixed and interred at Kensico Cemetery in Valhalla, New York. Instead, Eleanor decided it was best for the vase with her husband's ashes to be taken directly to Valhalla, where they remain today, along with hers.[93]

## NOTES

1. Dickey quoted in Gallico, *Pride of the Yankees*, 9–10.
2. Gehrig and Durso, *My Luke and I*, 210; and Robinson, *Iron Horse*, 244.
3. Gehrig and Durso, *My Luke and I*, 24; and Tofel, *Legend in the Making*, 31.
4. Tofel, *Legend in the Making*, 31.
5. Gallico, *Pride of the Yankees*, 13–14.
6. Joe DiMaggio quoted in Tofel, *Legend in the Making*, 31.
7. Tommy Henrich and Bill Glibert, *Five O'Clock Lightning: Ruth, Gehrig, DiMaggio, Mantle and the Glory Years of the New York Yankees* (New York: Crown, 1992), 64.
8. Robinson, *Iron Horse*, 245; and Tofel, *Legend in the Making*, 31.
9. Joe McCathy quoted in Joe Williams, "McCarthy Admits Doubt about Gehrig in '39 Yank Set Up," *New York World Telegram*, March 16, 1939.
10. Gehrig quoted in Robinson, *Iron Horse*, 245.
11. Vincent Flaherty quoted in Robinson, *Iron Horse*, 247.
12. McCarthy quoted in Robinson, *Iron Horse*, 248.
13. Robinson, *Iron Horse*, 249.
14. Williams and Prime, *Ted Williams' Hit List*, 65–66.
15. Robinson, *Iron Horse*, 249.
16. Ibid., 249–250.
17. James Kahn, "Gehrig Struggles at Plate," *New York Graphic*, April 25, 1939.
18. Bill Dickey quoted in Gallico, *Pride of the Yankees*, 14–16.
19. Gallico, *Pride of the Yankees*, 136.
20. Gehrig quoted in Dan Daniel, " 'Not Through!' Says Gehrig," *New York World Telegram*, April 28, 1939.
21. Ibid.

22. Robinson, *Iron Horse*, 250.
23. Honig, *Power Hitters*, 39.
24. Bak, *American Classic*, 153; and Robinson, *Iron Horse*, 251.
25. Gehrig quoted in Honig, *Power Hitters*, 39.
26. Robinson, *Iron Horse*, 251.
27. Gehrig and Durso, *My Luke and I*, 212–213.
28. Gehrig/McCarthy conversation quoted in Bak, *American Classic*, 153–154.
29. Harwell, "Wally Pipp's Big League Career Forgotten with a 'Headache,' " 58.
30. Bak, *American Classic*, 154.
31. Ibid.
32. George Selkirk quoted in Randy Schultz, "Gehrig Wasn't Defined by Streak," *Sporting News*, June 19, 1989.
33. Lou to Eleanor Gehrig, May 3, 1939, Detroit, MI, Gehrig Files, National Baseball Hall of Fame Library.
34. Joe McCarthy quoted in Robinson, *Iron Horse*, 255.
35. Gehrig and Durso, *My Luke and I*, 6–7.
36. Bak, *American Classic*, 155.
37. "Gehrig Ready for 'Check-up' " *New York Times*, June 13, 1939.
38. Bak, *American Classic*, 156.
39. Tofel, *Legend in the Making*, 114.
40. See Kathleen Wright, "Lou Gehrig's disease," in *Gale Encyclopedia of Alternative Medicine*, eds. Jacqueline L. Longe, and Deirdre S. Blanchfield (New York: Gale Group, 2002); Anne D. Walling, "Amyotrophic Lateral Sclerosis: Lou Gehrig's Disease," *American Family Physician*, March 15, 1999; and Edward Kasarskis and Mary Winslow, "When Did Lou Gehrig's Personal Illness Begin?" *Neurology*, 1989, 1243–1245.
41. Lou to Eleanor Gehrig, June 19, 1939, Rochester, MN, Gehrig Files, National Baseball Library.
42. Gehrig and Durso, *My Luke and I*, 11–13.
43. Ibid., 17.
44. Jimmy Powers, "Paralysis Ends Gehrig's Career," *New York Daily News*, June 22, 1939.
45. Ibid.; "Lou Gehrig Has Paralysis, Career with Yanks Ends," *Cleveland News*, June 22, 1939; and Whitney Martin, "Doctors Say Lou Must Retire to Conserve Energy," *Philadelphia Inquirer*, June 22, 1939.
46. Stanley Frank, "Tribute Paid to the Iron Horse Has No Equal in Baseball," *New York Times*, July 5, 1939.
47. Lou Gehrig quoted in Jack Miley, "Fun-Loving Guy Brings a Smile to Lou's Face," *New York Daily News*, July 5, 1939.
48. Bak, *American Classic*, 158.
49. Ibid., 159.
50. Joe McCarthy quoted in Tofel, *Legend in the Making*, 140.
51. Bak, *American Classic*, 160.
52. Ibid., 160–161.

53. Ibid., 161.

54. Ruth, *Babe Ruth Story*, 218–219; and Smelser, *Life That Ruth Built*, 524.

55. Eleanor Gehrig quoted in Pollack interview. Eleanor also harbored some bitterness against the Yankees for many years, telling others that "all I got was a tea set that costs $5 a month to keep polished." See Eleanor Gehrig quoted in Tom Weir, "Gehrig's Wife Left Legacy of Uncommon Memories," *USA Today*, September 1, 1995.

56. Shirley Povich, " 'Iron Horse' Breaks as Athletic Greats Meet in His Honor," *Washington Post*, July 5, 1939.

57. "Lou Gehrig Named to the Hall of Fame," *New York Daily News*, December 8, 1939.

58. "No Other Player to Use Gehrig's Number or Locker," *New York Times*, January 6, 1940.

59. Lou Gehrig quoted in Graham, *Quiet Hero*, 224–225.

60. Robinson, *Iron Horse*, 260.

61. Edward T. Murphy, "Gehrig Proves Real Iron Man as He Fights to Overcome Ailment," *New York Sun*, June 22, 1939.

62. Mayo doctors and Lou Gehrig quoted in *Rochester (MN) Post-Bulletin*, August 22, 1939.

63. Lou Gehrig quoted in interview with Dwight Merriam, Rochester, MN, August 22, 1939. Transcribed by Jeremy Jones in *Memories and Dreams*, 25, no. 2, Spring 2003, 16–17.

64. Ibid.

65. Conversation between Gehrig and Selkirk quoted in Graham, *Quiet Hero*, 225.

66. Graham, *Quiet Hero*, 211.

67. Gallagher and LaConte, *Yankee Encyclopedia*, 389.

68. Barrow quoted in Weir, "Gehrig's Wife Left Legacy."

69. Robinson, *Iron Horse*, 261–262.

70. Robinson, "Lou Gehrig: Columbia Legend and American Hero," 6–7. Fiorello La Guardia (1882–1947) was the first of New York City's modern mayors to serve three four-year terms. As a congressman and mayor, he was a spokesman for urban America and played a significant role in redefining the relationship between America's cities and the federal government. See Alyn Brodsky, *The Great Mayor: Fiorello La Guardia and the Making of the City of New York* (New York: St. Martin's Press, 2003).

71. Gehrig and Durso, *My Luke and I*, 18–19.

72. Ibid., 20.

73. Bak, *American Classic*, 163–164.

74. Lou Gehrig quoted in Graham, *Quiet Hero*, 238; and Robinson, "Lou Gehrig: Columbia Legend and American Hero," 7.

75. Graham, *Quiet Hero*, 239–240.

76. Mel Allen quoted in Leo Trachtenberg, *The Wonder Team: The True Story of the Incomparable 1927 New York Yankees* (Bowling Green, OH: Bowling Green State University Popular Press, 1995), 58–59.

77. Gehrig and Durso, *My Luke and I*, 49–50.

78. Ibid., 21.

79. "Physicians Baffled by 'Gehrig's Disease,'" *New York World Telegram*, June 4, 1941; and Bob Considine, "John Kieran: Sage of Rockport," *Boston Herald American*, April 18, 1975.

80. Tom Watson, "Dying Yankee Legend Came Here to Help Kids," *Riverdale Press*, June 8, 1989.

81. Jimmy Powers, "Has 'Polio' Hit the Yankees?" *New York Daily News*, August 18, 1940.

82. Jimmy Powers, "Our Apologies to Lou Gehrig and the Yankees," *New York Daily News*, September 26, 1940.

83. Kieran quoted in Considine, "John Kieran: Sage of Rockport."

84. Tommy Henrich quoted in Brett Topel, "Yankee Teammates Recall the Greatness of Lou Gehrig," *Baseball Digest*, July 1995, 29; See also "Gehrig Thinks He Is Winning," *New York World Telegram*, January 30, 1941.

85. Bill Dickey quoted in Gallico, *Pride of the Yankees*, 17.

86. Gehrig and Durso, *My Luke and I*, 226; and Eleanor Gehrig quoted in Milton Richman, "Mrs. Gehrig Likes to Talk about Lou," *New York Times*, August 8, 1973.

87. Graham, *Quiet Hero*, 249.

88. Ibid., 249–250; and "Gehrig, Iron Man of Baseball Dies at the Age of 37," *New York Times*, June 3, 1941.

89. Dick McCann, "Gehrig Funeral This Morning," *New York Daily News*, June 4, 1941; and interview with Evelyn Davies, Riverdale, New York, June 10, 2003.

90. Tofel, *Legend in the Making*, 270.

91. Reverend Gerald V. Barry quoted in Robinson, *Iron Horse*, 273.

92. Bill Dickey quoted in ibid.

93. Pollack interview.

8

# Making of a Legend, 1941–2002

After Lou's death, Eleanor devoted her life to preserving his memory. Her efforts went far beyond those of protecting his name. She became the classic "baseball widow," actively promoting an image of Lou as a prototype of the clean-living, all-American hero and, later, as a champion in the fight against ALS, the disease that came to bear his name. At various times, her efforts enjoyed the support of Major League Baseball, of Hollywood, and of the medical community.

The apotheosis of Gehrig began shortly after his death, when his gravesite at Kensico Cemetery became a popular tourist attraction. Fans, sightseers, and picnickers would leave balls, bats, and handwritten letters at Lou's grave as tributes to the Iron Horse. The gravesite was so besieged by an overzealous public that there was at least one attempt to steal the vase containing Gehrig's ashes, which were locked inside the tombstone.[1] Eleanor and her in-laws quickly grew frustrated with the situation and offered Lou's ashes to the National Baseball Hall of Fame. The Hall, "deeply impressed by the offer," immediately began to explore the legal implications of a museum serving as a repository for human remains and secretly drafted plans for a "Tomb of Baseball's Immortals."[2] Debate over the exact nature of the memorial continued for several years, with plans ranging from a small, intimate crypt beneath Gehrig's bronze plaque to a large-scale mausoleum.[3]

Other tributes were less sensational. The Yankees, who had already retired Gehrig's uniform number and sealed his locker, erected a centerfield monument to the fallen star and renamed the concourse at their stadium "Gehrig Plaza."

Major League Baseball honored Lou by dedicating the 1941 World Series to his memory.[4]

The Japanese attack on Pearl Harbor and the coming of World War II offered a fertile environment for further cultivation of the Gehrig legend. At a time when the U.S. government was asking the American people to sacrifice for the country, Gehrig's patriotism, selfless example, and courage offered a ready-made hero for the war effort. Foster Field, an army–air force base in Victoria, Texas, was quick to make the connection by naming an athletic field in Lou's honor, and was the first branch of the military to do so.[5] Shortly after, a merchant marine troop transport ship was named in his honor. Commissioned in 1943, the Liberty ship *Lou Gehrig* carried 480 men and 120 vehicles and was involved in Operation Neptune one year later. It also landed in Normandy thirteen days after D-Day in June 1944.[6]

Eleanor, in an attempt to link her husband's memory with the American cause, promoted war bond drives. She raised more than $6 million by auctioning off some of Lou's memorabilia, including one of his MVP trophies. Believing that the trophy would bring at most "ten to fifteen thousand dollars," she was astonished when the Southland Life Insurance Company of Dallas, Texas, offered $1 million for it.[7] In addition, Eleanor joined the Red Cross Motor Corps and drove sick and disabled people who couldn't ride New York City buses or subways to clinics and hospitals. Her efforts were recognized by President Franklin D. Roosevelt, who invited her for a visit to the presidential retreat in Warm Springs, Georgia.[8]

Several biographies, published in the years immediately following Gehrig's death, reinforced the late Yankee slugger's image as an all-American hero. Stanley W. Carlson's *Lou Gehrig: Baseball's Iron Man*, Richard G. Hubler's *Lou Gehrig: Iron Horse of Baseball*, Frank Graham's *Lou Gehrig: A Quiet Hero*, and Paul Gallico's *Lou Gehrig: Pride of the Yankees* are all affectionate tributes to a fallen hero designed to inspire young readers with a model of courage, perseverance, and loyalty. While all these biographies are handy, quick-reading accounts of the Iron Horse's life, Graham and Gallico provide many lively conversations that may have been embellished by these sportswriters.[9] Gallico's book was the most popular, probably because he told Gehrig's story in the context of the American Dream, explaining that "it was the American public that made Lou Gehrig a national hero":

> Because what happened to Gehrig, his life, his struggles, his one love and his ending, far transcends that evanescent, glittering surface stuff called "color". . . . He entered the hearts of the American people because of his living as well as his passing, he became and was to

> the end, a great and splendid human being. His is an American story, a boy of foreign-born parents who rose from poverty to dignity and success, and his virtues are the virtues that are admired by the American people and which in the past have helped to guide us.[10]

To be sure, Gehrig's example resonated with the common person because Gehrig was a "gamer," someone who went to work each day, put his back to the wheel for his family, and never complained. With patriotic fervor at its height, Gehrig's story was the stuff of box office smashes, or so believed Niven Busch, the executive producer for Goldwyn films.

When Busch first suggested the idea of a bio-pic on Gehrig to his boss, Sam Goldwyn, the movie mogul rejected it. Goldwyn, a Polish Jew who had immigrated to the United States at age 19, knew little of the American love affair with baseball. "It's box office poison," he told Busch. "If people want baseball, they go to the ballpark."[11] But when Busch showed his boss a newsreel of Gehrig's farewell speech, Goldwyn was noticeably moved and convinced that such a film had potential in the current climate. Granted permission to proceed, Busch paid Eleanor Gehrig $30,000 for rights to the story and hired Paul Gallico to write the screenplay. The movie would be titled *Pride of the Yankees*, after Gallico's book.[12]

Actual ballplayers were hired for the supporting roles. Babe Ruth was invited to play himself in the film. Having suffered two mild heart attacks in the previous year, the Bambino was not in good health and weighed about 270 pounds. But he eagerly accepted the invitation and dieted to make himself presentable, losing nearly forty pounds in a few months. Although the weight loss made him irritable, Ruth proved to be a natural in front of the camera. He became so caught up in reliving the mayhem of a pennant-clinching celebration that he put his fist through the window of a Pullman car.[13] Bill Dickey, Mark Koenig, Tony Lazzeri, and Bob Meusel were also invited to play themselves and accepted.[14]

Teresa Wright, then Busch's girlfriend, played Eleanor Gehrig. Wright had worked for Goldwyn before in the screen adaptation of "The Little Foxes" and was in the midst of a slow but steady rise to stardom. At 5 feet, 2 inches and 110 pounds, the 22-year-old actress matched Eleanor's stature, but she had reservations about taking the role, wondering if audiences would accept her as an older woman.[15] Busch convinced her otherwise and she would later receive an Oscar nomination for the role.

Deciding on an actor to play Lou was much more difficult. Christy Walsh, Gehrig's former publicist, suggested a nationwide search. Among those considered were Eddie Albert, Dennis Morgan, Spencer Tracy, Pat O'Brien, and John Wayne.[16] But Goldwyn believed that only Gary Cooper could play the "everyman" role while still bringing recognizable star appeal to the film. Cooper, fresh from winning an Academy Award for *Sergeant York*, accepted the $150,000 offer to play the role.[17]

Although Cooper possessed all the necessary character attributes to play Lou Gehrig and he was made to look younger than his 41 years, he knew very little about how to hit or throw a baseball and he was right-handed. Goldwyn hired former Yankee Lefty O'Doul to tutor him. Still, Cooper was not very convincing and had to be doubled by Babe Herman, a former Brooklyn Dodger, in some of the distant camera shots. Goldwyn solved the right-handed actor's problem of portraying a left-handed power hitter in the post-production process by reversing the film to make Cooper appear left-handed. The actor's swings were also artificially sped up to make them appear more powerful than they actually were.[18]

Eleanor's involvement was critical to the success of the film. She loaned her husband's trophies and scrapbooks of newspaper clippings for the film, as well as a gold bracelet given to her by Lou on their fourth wedding anniversary.[19] Her suggestions were also welcomed by cast members and the producers and she enjoyed sharing her thoughts about the production in phone conversations with Christy Walsh.[20] "I know she was very happy with the film," said Teresa Wright about Eleanor's reception of *Pride of the Yankees*. "I think it meant a lot to her. With the sadness of Lou's early death, I think, in a way, it gave him back to her for a while. Having her on the set occasionally, where she was so warm, friendly and supportive only helped."[21]

*Pride of the Yankees* premiered in July 1942 in New York City and then was distributed across the nation. While the film took a number of liberties with Lou's private life, it was hugely successful at the box office.[22] The movie grossed more than $3 million and was one of the top-ten moneymakers of the year.[23] The film was nominated for eleven Academy Awards in 1943, and both Wright and Cooper received Oscar nominations for their performances. The popularity of *Pride of the Yankees* immortalized Gehrig in a way that few other films have enhanced the lives of their subjects and it is still widely regarded as one of the finest baseball movies ever made.[24]

In the meantime, a nasty conflict over Lou's will and whether or not to relocate his remains was brewing between Eleanor and her in-laws. Although Gehrig bequeathed all his trophies to his parents, he left an estate of $171,251 and some 1,085 shares of stock to Eleanor and his attorney, Milton Eisenberg. In his will, Gehrig stipulated that the stocks be used for investment or income and the interest be used to pay $5 per month to his parents, an amount that would supplement the $200-per-month income they already received from a $20,000 life insurance policy he had taken out when he got married to Eleanor. The balance of the income from the stock would be paid to Eleanor, who was made executrix of his will.[25] But the Gehrigs accused their daughter-in-law of withholding payments on the income generated from Lou's insurance policy and brought suit against her in August 1943 for the sum of $5,188.53.[26] The suit was quickly settled out of court, but it left both parties with hard feelings toward each other.[27]

At the same time, Eleanor was growing frustrated with the deteriorating condition of Lou's gravesite, where the grass was "shoddy and worn out from frequent trespassing."[28] She continued to hope that the Hall of Fame would accept her husband's ashes until 1949, when a report of the intended transfer appeared in the New York newspapers. Angered by the leak, she put all plans on hold. Another heated disagreement between Eleanor and her in-laws followed, but as executor of the estate her decision prevailed. Lou's ashes would remain at Kensico, to the dismay of his parents, who died in the mid-1950s.[29]

After World War II, Eleanor devoted her energies to raising money to find a cure for ALS. There was no better way to vindicate her loss than by finding a cure to the illness that had claimed her husband's life. Her efforts would ensure that the fight against ALS would be forever linked to Lou Gehrig's name and legacy. When the Muscular Dystrophy Association of America was formed in 1950, Eleanor became National Campaign Chairman, making frequent fund-raising trips in major cities across the nation.[30] She urged Congress to finance a campaign against multiple sclerosis to stimulate research. "To watch someone close to you become a helpless paralytic," she said, testifying before a Congressional hearing, "and to know that medical science is powerless to halt the progress of the disease is something no person should be called upon to endure."[31] Eleanor also enlisted the assistance of Senators Charles W. Tobey (Republican—New Hampshire) and Joseph C. O'Mahoney (Democrat—Wyoming) to co-author a bipartisan bill to establish a national institute for multiple sclerosis research.[32] All these efforts were undertaken to ensure that Lou's name would only be associated with constructive causes rather than be exploited for commercial purposes.

With Eleanor's blessing, Lou continued to be memorialized in the 1950s. Eleanor was especially pleased that Yankee broadcaster Mel Allen established a scholarship in Lou's name at Columbia University for financially needy students.[33] Similarly, she encouraged the creation of an annual "Lou Gehrig Award" by the Phi Delta Theta Fraternity of Oxford, Ohio; the award was given to the major leaguer who best exemplified her husband's intangible qualities.[34] Among the first recipients of the award were Alvin Dark of the New

York Giants, Peewee Reese of the Brooklyn Dodgers, and Stan Musial of the St. Louis Cardinals.[35] But in the early 1960s, when a liquor company made plans to promote its brand of scotch by using the Iron Horse's image, Eleanor hired George Pollack, a New York City trial lawyer, to stop them.

"The scotch ad campaign talked about the 'perfect blend of champions' and used photos of Lou and Babe Ruth," recalled Pollack. "Eleanor hired me to stop the ad, pointing out that Lou never drank hard liquor."[36] Pollack realized that there was nothing he could do legally because, at the time, commercial use of a deceased celebrity's name or image was permissible. But he still wrote a letter to the attorneys representing the liquor company and informed them that he was applying for an injunction to halt their action.

"What a pity," Pollack wrote, "to tarnish the memory of a beloved athlete who never drank just to advertise your cheap scotch." A few days later he received a phone call from a young lawyer whose firm represented the scotch company.

"You sound like you're experienced, Mr. Pollack," he began, patronizingly. "I'm sure you realize that our client's use of the Gehrig image is, in fact, legal. There's nothing you can do to stop it."

Unbeknownst to the lawyer, Pollack had done some trial work with the firm and knew the senior partner well.

"You show my letter to your boss, and let's see what he says," countered Pollack. Within the next few hours the phone rang again. This time it was the head of the firm. "George, you wouldn't block the scotch ad, would you?"

"Jim, I have no alternative but to go public with this," replied Pollack.

"How much does your client want?"

"She doesn't want any money," he said. "She just wants to stop the advertisement."

Not wanting the negative publicity, the company withdrew the scotch ad. Eleanor was so grateful for Pollack's intercession that she retained his legal services on all matters regarding Lou's name, image, and reputation.[37]

By the mid-1970s, Eleanor's parents and brother had passed away. Because she had never remarried, Pollack became her close friend and confidant, eventually being named the executor of her estate. She trusted the middle-aged lawyer, probably because she saw a similarity between him and her late husband. Pollack, like Lou, came from humble beginnings. Both men were born and raised in the Yorkville section of Manhattan, where a polyglot culture of immigrant Irish, Germans, and Jews cultivated in their children the intangible virtues of industry, perseverance, and helping others. Pollack attended the city's public schools and then went on to St. John's University, where he held down two jobs to pay the tuition. In 1938, he graduated from St. John's Law School and became a trial lawyer in New York City's appellate court system.[38] While he was not an especially big fan of baseball, Pollack was extremely committed to his clients, and Eleanor was aware of both of these qualities, which endeared him to her even more. Pollack, on the other hand, had tremendous admiration for Eleanor's deep devotion to the memory of her late husband. "Theirs was a truly great love affair," he said. "She never married, never even dated after Lou's death. How could she? Who else could measure up to such an adored figure as Lou. Eleanor was content to lead a lonely life because she saw her role as preserving his legend."[39]

Eleanor Gehrig did lead a lonely life, eased only by reading, listening to operas, occasional trips to Old Timers' Day games at Yankee Stadium, and binge drinking. When Pollack discovered the drinking problem, he encouraged her to write a book about her marriage, believing that it would allow her to relive some of the happier times in her life. Sportswriter Joe Durso agreed to assist her in a collaborative book entitled, *My Luke and I*, published in 1976. But the book was *not* a ghost effort—Eleanor had writing talent and the success of the book was due to its conversational style.[40] This short volume is more of a reminiscence than a biography and as much her story as his. But Eleanor also provides some keen insights into her husband's personality, work ethic, and idiosyncrasies. Her writing demonstrated the same sense of personal integrity that characterized her husband. Although she might have raised sales of the book by writing the kind of "kiss-and-tell" account that was so popular during the 1970s, she refused to compromise herself.[41] Throughout the book, Eleanor offers the reader an unmistakable sense of the love and devotion the couple had for each other. Her ability to express the nature of their relationship in an exceptionally moving way is reflected in the concluding paragraphs, where she admits the following:

> Though the summers have come and gone, there has been no comfort from the thought of basking as a professional widow and there has been no comfort from the thought of another man, as in his case there could have been no thought of another woman. Loneliness, yes; even emptiness. But I had an "answer" to those six years of towering joy followed by those two years of ruin. . . . I would not have traded two minutes of the joy and the grief with that man for two decades of anything with another. Happy or sad, filled with great expectations, or great frustration, we had attained it for whatever brief instant that fate had decided. The most in life, the unattainable, and we were not star-crossed by it. We were blessed with it, my Luke and I.[42]

The book was so successful that it inspired a television movie. Once again, Pollack had to intercede to make the film possible.

According to an earlier contract Eleanor signed with MGM Studios for *Pride of the Yankees,* she was prohibited from making a film about her own life. Pollack would have to secure a release from MGM. Bill Shea, a politician-lawyer and part-owner of the New York Mets, offered to handle the matter, confident that he could save Eleanor the considerable expense involved in copyright law. "It won't cost you a nickel," he boasted to Pollack. As it turned out, Shea's intercession cost Eleanor $35,000.

A few months later, Pollack took Eleanor to an Old Timer's Day Game at Yankee Stadium and at the post-game dinner ran into Shea, who was with a federal judge and his wife. When he saw the two of them, Shea blurted out, "There's George Pollack who stole Eleanor Gehrig away from me as a client!"

Pollack slowly approached the trio. "Bill, I know you represent many people for nothing at all, God bless you," he said, with a twinkle in his eye. "But I got news for you—I do it for less!"[43]

The television movie was titled *A Love Affair: The Eleanor and Lou Gehrig Story* and starred Blythe Danner as Eleanor and Edward Herrmann as Lou. Danner was especially convincing in her role, but Herrmann worried before filming began that he didn't bring much to his role. "What made it so tough was that I could find no 'key' to [Lou's] character," he admitted. "There was no strangeness, there was nothing spectacular about him. As Eleanor told me, he was just a 'square, honest guy.' "[44]

To be sure, *A Love Affair,* which premiered on NBC on January 15, 1978, was burdened by many factors, not the least of which was Herrmann's understated performance. Too many flashbacks made it difficult for viewers to follow an accurate chronology of events, and the 1970s-style haircuts made it difficult to believe that the story took place largely in the 1920s and 1930s. But true to the film's title, *A Love Affair* is indeed a love story in which baseball plays an almost incidental part and gives Eleanor's perspective of the couple's relationship its just due. Unfortunately, the movie never touched a large viewing audience. Originally scheduled to air on October 9, 1977, the movie was preempted by a World Series game and was rescheduled for January 15, 1978, when it competed with the first nighttime Super Bowl.[45] Nevertheless, *A Love Affair* was probably the highlight of Eleanor's old age.

She lead a quiet and lonely life in her East Side apartment and as she grew older her drinking became more severe. But she was extremely careful to keep the indiscretion private so as not to tarnish the Gehrig legend. Eleanor also became estranged from the few friends she had left. "Near the end of her life," said George Pollack, "I became worried when she didn't return my phone calls.

Once I had to call the superintendent of her apartment building to gain entry. I found her out cold with a bottle of whiskey beside her." Pollack rushed Eleanor to Columbia Presbyterian Hospital and waited for three hours until she was sober. When she realized what he had done, Eleanor was both embarrassed and touched by her friend's concern. The two of them sat in the waiting room in silence, not knowing what to say.

Suddenly Eleanor snapped, "You've never seen me drunk, have you George?"

"Passed out? Yes," replied Pollack with a poker face. "Drunk? Never."[46] After that, Pollack hired a nurse to stay with Eleanor, despite her protestations. Still, when she was left alone, Eleanor could be very careless. She almost burned herself to death in 1982 when she fell asleep with a lighted cigarette in bed and her apartment caught fire.[47] Finally, on March 7, 1984, Eleanor Gehrig passed away in her sleep at the age of 79.[48]

Like Lou, she requested that her remains be cremated, the ashes mixed with his and placed inside the tombstone at Kensico Cemetery. Pollack tried to honor those wishes. He had her remains cremated and placed in a small urn and then drove them up to Kensico. When he and his wife, Dorothy, arrived at the cemetery, they noticed that the caretakers had erected a large tent in anticipation of a celebrity's funeral service. Sadly, no one else was there. The Pollacks were Eleanor's only remaining friends. George knelt down, removed the key that Eleanor had given him from his pocket, and opened the small brass doors on the face of the tombstone. He carefully studied the small urn inside containing Lou's ashes and remembered his client's last request to mix her ashes with his so they could be reunited eternally. But this was one request her executor could not bring himself to fulfill. Instead, Pollack placed Eleanor's urn alongside that of her husband, shut and locked the brass doors, and returned home to the city. There would have to be other ways to honor her wishes.[49]

In her will, Eleanor bequeathed all the baseball-related objects she inherited after Lou's death—a total of forty-eight items—to the National Baseball Hall of Fame in Cooperstown, New York.[50] Together with the additional thirty-five items left by Christina Gehrig at her death in 1956, the Hall of Fame inherited a total of eighty-three objects, including Gehrig's first and last baseball gloves, several trophies, eight commemorative baseballs, and more than a dozen photographs.[51]

At least one of Lou's gloves escaped the Hall of Fame's collection. Barry Halper, part-owner of the Yankees and a prominent sports memorabilia dealer, purchased a Gehrig glove for $25,000 from Babe Dahlgren, the Yankee who replaced Lou at first base in 1939.[52] The glove was later coveted by President George Bush, Sr., who idolized the Iron Horse while he was a student-athlete at Andover Academy and, later, when he was captain of Yale University's baseball team. Once, when asked by a baseball writer if he could have any piece of memorabilia, what would it be, the president replied, "Lou Gehrig's first baseman's mitt. I would love to have that." The remark caught the attention of Bush's White House aides, who hoped to obtain the glove as a gift to the president.

In 1989, while Bush was in the Mediterranean meeting with Russian prime minister Mikhail Gorbachev, his staff embarked on a quest to find one of Gehrig's gloves. White House secretary Jan Burmeister began the search by contacting the National Baseball Hall of Fame, which has two of the gloves in their collections. Informing her that neither item was obtainable, the Hall's staff suggested she contact George Pollack, who was considered to be the only person who could fulfill such an extraordinary request. Burmeister immediately called the former trial lawyer to make the request for Bush.

"Is this *really* important to the president?" Pollack asked. "Because I'm a registered Democrat!"

"Yes," she replied.

After a brief hesitation, Pollack, having considered what constituted a patriotic duty, said, "Well, if its important to the president I will try to help you."

Pollack contacted Halper and explained the situation. Bush's aides had no intention of purchasing the glove. Instead they were hoping that the president's interest alone would convince Halper to make a gift of it. To be sure, Halper considered the glove one of his most prized possessions, but he was intrigued by Bush's interest. Pollack, on the other hand, wanted to generate publicity for the Gehrig name to heighten the public awareness of ALS research and raise more money for it. To persuade Halper to make the deal, the executor of the Gehrig estate promised him that "whatever value you place on the glove, it would be assessed that way."

Halper agreed on the condition that Pollack would accompany him to Washington to present the glove to the president. Pollack consented to the request and informed the White House staff that they could expect to receive the glove.

But the next day Halper phoned Pollack with another condition: the president would have to come to his house for dinner. At first Pollack thought he was joking. But as the conversation continued, he realized that the wealthy young man was serious.

"Look George, I'm just interested in having dinner with the president," explained Halper. "I'm not interested in the publicity like you are."

Without missing a beat, Pollack retorted, "Sure Barry, who'll know that Bush is at your house when all those secret servicemen invade the neighborhood!" Nevertheless, he phoned Burmeister and informed her of Halper's request. Instead of rejecting the dinner invitation outright as he expected, she actually held out the possibility that the president would accept the next time he traveled to New York.

Halper was overjoyed. He sent the president a videotape featuring his extensive baseball memorabilia collection, including the Gehrig glove. A few days later, the president wrote a letter thanking him for his generosity and informing him that he could not accept the Gehrig glove. Like all gifts to the president, the glove would belong to the office, not the individual who held it. Disappointed by news, Halper understood Bush's position and put the issue to rest, but Pollack refused to allow such an extraordinary opportunity to publicize the Gehrig legend slip away.

He approached Halper with another idea. Why not contact the president's son, George W. Bush, then-owner of the Texas Rangers, and make a symbolic presentation of the glove to the White House the next time the Rangers came to New York to play the Yankees? That way the president would be happy, Halper could keep the glove, and Pollack would generate the publicity he wanted. Negotiations took place for several weeks, but the presentation never occurred. The glove was sold at an auction a decade later for more than $200,000 as part of the Halper Collection, which in total brought an estimated $15 million.[53]

In addition to the glove, other Gehrig items in the collection included the number 4 home jersey in which the Iron Horse delivered his farewell-to-baseball address, bats, and several autographed baseballs and photos. "Gehrig memorabilia is the most difficult to obtain," insists Halper, who admits to a personal fascination with the late Yankee slugger's autograph. "It's a graceful signature, which is almost always preceded by the words, 'cordially yours,' " he explains. "The autograph is very much a reflection of his education. Few people realize that Gehrig was taught to write with his right hand in elementary school and continued to write with that hand, even though he did everything else left-handed. That's probably why the letters of his signature are very close and tight. He took great care and pride in writing it."[54]

The dearness of Gehrig memorabilia only seemed to enhance the public fascination with the Iron Horse. The last decade, in particular, has witnessed another rash of Gehrig biographies. Ray Robinson's *Iron Horse: Lou Gehrig in His Time*, published in 1990, is widely considered by baseball historians as the seminal account of Gehrig's life. This carefully researched biography portrays the Yankee slugger as shy and unassuming but also every bit the hero as his more flamboyant teammate, Babe Ruth. Robinson details Gehrig's life and career with an insightful perspective on baseball during the 1920s and the Depression era.[55]

In 1995, Richard Bak compiled an illustrated biography entitled *Lou Gehrig: An American Classic*. Bak offers readers an engaging narrative that fixes Gehrig nicely into the context of the time period in which he lived. With more than 250 photographs (many rarely seen), this attractive coffee-table book draws on personal letters and interviews of Gehrig contemporaries, among other sources.[56]

In 2002, Richard J. Tofel contributed another fine work to the growing literature on Gehrig. Although not a biography, Tofel's *A Legend in the Making: The New York Yankees in 1939* chronicles the slow, painful decline of the Iron Horse in his final major league season. This day-to-day account of the 1939 campaign paints a moving portrait of Gehrig, who, in spite of his failing body, managed to conduct himself with extraordinary courage and grace.[57]

In addition, several juvenile biographies of the Iron Horse were penned during the 1990s, including David A. Adler's *Lou Gehrig: The Luckiest Man*; Norman L. Macht's *Lou Gehrig*, part of the Chelsea House "Baseball Legends" series; and Richard Rambeck's *Lou Gehrig*.[58] With their action photographs, bright illustrations, and entertaining narratives, these juvenile biographies provide a wonderful introduction to the Iron Horse for young children.

Today there are more than a dozen biographies of Lou Gehrig, insuring that his major league career and exemplary behavior will always be part of the historical record. But the Iron Horse's more enduring legacy can be found in the fight against amyotrophic lateral sclerosis. When Eleanor Gehrig passed away in 1984, she left $100,000 to Columbia Presbyterian Hospital and an additional $100,000 to the Rip Van Winkle Fund for ALS research.[59] Shortly after her death, Pollack, now executor of the Gehrig estate, in accordance with Eleanor's last wishes, began to explore ways to increase the $200,000 bequest by raising money for ALS research. To that end, he signed a licensing agreement with the Curtis Management Group of Indianapolis, Indiana, to cover all merchandise with Lou's name or image, with the profits going to both of the foundations named in Eleanor's will.[60] "My hope," Pollack told the press, is that Lou's name and image can provide the money to some day find a cure for ALS. That would be simple justice."[61]

True to his word, Pollack, who prides himself as an "old-fashioned lawyer" whose commitment to his clients "extends beyond the grave," has spent the last two decades raising money for that cure. "If you are the executor of an estate," he explains, "you have certain higher responsibilities that I believe you owe to your clients, whether they are dead or alive. Since Eleanor's death then, I've devoted myself to perpetuating the Gehrig legend because that's what she would want."[62] Indeed, Pollack has become the caretaker of the Gehrig legend.

Cal Ripken's quest to break Iron Horse's consecutive-game streak in 1995 provided a wonderful opportunity for the cause. Although Ripken played for the Baltimore Orioles, not the Yankees, he shared some remarkable similarities with the Iron Horse. Both men spent their entire careers with one team, both possessed quiet and self-effacing personalities, and both played without complaint through batting slumps, illnesses, and the various nagging pains that come with advanced age. But the Orioles' future Hall-of-Famer downplays any comparison. "Lou Gehrig was one of the greatest figures in all of baseball," he said in a recent interview. "I have to remind other people that breaking his consecutive game streak doesn't mean that my abilities should be compared to his. So even to be mentioned in the same breath as Lou is quite a compliment." Still, Ripken admitted that he shared Gehrig's "passion for the game and team commitment," qualities he believes can be attributed to a "strong sense of responsibility and personal pride."[63]

To be sure, if Gehrig represented the best of the past, Ripken certainly represents the best of the present. He possesses a refreshing sense of humility and respect for the game that resonated with fans throughout his quest to set the new consecutive-game record. Unlike Roger Maris and Henry Aaron, who felt the pressure of chasing the ghost of Babe Ruth, Ripken chose to look at his quest as a "celebration of baseball that linked the Golden Age of the game and one of its heroes to the present."[64] He also made sure to honor Gehrig whenever possible. On the eve of his record-breaking game, for example, when New York sportswriters asked Ripken whether Gehrig was bigger than the consecutive-game record, the Orioles' shortstop replied, "Was Lou Gehrig obsessed with the streak? Did the Yankees want his record to continue? I don't know. Put the streak aside. Gehrig was one of the very best baseball players who ever played."[65] Pollack was impressed with Ripken, whom he considered "much like Lou himself—a straight arrow guy, and a team player who works hard." He told the press, "I may be wrong, but I think it's better for Lou Gehrig that Cal Ripken breaks his record. It will bring him back to life for so many people who never saw him play."[66] In fact, Ripken's quest to break Gehrig's consecutive-game streak did more to raise money for ALS research than anyone anticipated.

By September 1995, the ALS fund at Columbia Presbyterian Hospital, fed by the Gehrig licensing contract, amounted to $332,000, much of it raised over the previous few years as Ripken drew closer to Lou's record. Plans had been made to use the money to renovate an entire floor of the hospital's Neurological Institute for an "Eleanor and Lou Gehrig Muscular Dystrophy/ALS Center," something that would cost an estimated $1.5 to $2 million.[67] While Pollack continued his own efforts to see those plans come to fruition, the Baltimore Orioles were making some plans of their own. Team owner Peter

Angelos set a $1 million goal for ALS research at Johns Hopkins University Hospital during Ripken's quest. To help reach that goal, the Orioles announced that they would sell 260 cushioned folding chairs, placed in rows of two in front of the left and right field grandstands for September 6, 1995, the night that Ripken was scheduled to break Gehrig's record at Baltimore's Camden Yards. Each folding chair was emblazoned with a special logo marking the occasion and sold for $5,000. Buyers would not only have the opportunity to see Ripken break the record, but also to take the chair home with them as a souvenir of the occasion and be invited back for a special reception hosted by Ripken himself. The Orioles also set up a giant tent to educate the public about ALS and accept donations for the fight against the debilitating disease.[68]

When Ripken broke the record on September 6, the game was interrupted during the sixth inning—the point at which the game was official—for a ceremony. In his remarks to the crowd, the Orioles shortstop spoke from the heart about his achievement and what it meant to him. "Whether your name is Gehrig or Ripken, or that of some youngster who picks up his bat or puts on his glove, you are challenged by the game of baseball to do your very best, day in and day out," he said. "And that's all I've ever tried to do."[69] Cal Ripken had given the fans more than a new record; he showed a younger generation the importance of perseverance and humility. Lou Gehrig would have been proud. Pollack certainly was. "I had tears in my eyes the moment that game was official," he recalled. "I knew that both Lou and Eleanor would be happy for Cal. In fact, Eleanor often told me that 'records are made to be broken.' I also knew that that event would allow Lou to live forever."[70] If finding a cure for ALS would give Gehrig immortality, Ripken's achievement resulted in a hefty financial contribution toward that goal. The night he broke the record, the Orioles raised $1.3 million. Angelos was so happy with the results that during the mid-game ceremony, he announced that his team would contribute another $700,000 to ALS research, raising the total figure to $2 million.[71]

Cal Ripken would go on to play every Orioles game for more than three years before taking himself out of the line-up on September 20, 1998. His record of 2,632 consecutive games may never be broken.[72] But the achievement seems to have only enhanced Gehrig's legend. In 1996, Hall-of-Famer Ted Williams, the last player to hit .400, ranked Gehrig second behind Babe Ruth on his list of baseball's all-time greatest hitters. He added that Gehrig might have finished first "if he could have played out his career in good health."[73] Three years later, in 1999, when Major League Baseball selected its "All-Century Team," Gehrig was voted by the fans as the top first baseman of the twentieth century. With the focus now off his consecutive game streak, Gehrig was appreciated for his tremendous accomplishments during those 2,130 games, which included seven 150-RBI seasons, eight 200-hit seasons, and three seasons in which his slugging percentage was .700 or better.[74] Similar honors were awarded by the *Sporting News*, which named Gehrig the sixth best player of all time, and *Baseball Digest*, which named him the fifth best player of all time.[75] In 2002, Major League Baseball recognized the Iron Horse's farewell address as one of the top ten moments in baseball history.

Today, Lou Gehrig's legend continues to raise money for ALS research. George Pollack has discovered more creative methods of fund-raising, although some have earned him harsh criticism from baseball purists. In 2001, for example, the former trial lawyer signed a lucrative agreement with Alcatel, a French telecommunications company, for the rights to use Gehrig's famous farewell speech as part of an advertising campaign that asks viewers what would happen if there were no audiences to hear the ideas in famous speeches. An earlier commercial showing the Reverend Dr. Martin Luther King, Jr., delivering his "I Have a Dream" speech to an empty Washington Mall in 1963 outraged civil rights leaders, who believed that King's image and words were being exploited. Similarly, Alcatel digitally altered scenes of Gehrig's farewell address to have him speaking to an empty Yankee Stadium.[76]

Critics of the commercial argue that it exploits Gehrig by suggesting that his remarks were not important enough to be heard by anyone. Others are insulted by Alcatel's exploitation of an American hero who experienced a tragic and untimely death, calling the ad "macabre commercial exploitation."[77] But Brad Burns, senior vice-president for corporate communications at Alcatel, defended the ad. "It's our intention to honor Lou Gehrig," he explained. "Our commercial is designed to make viewers question, 'What if those powerful words did not connect with people?' In doing so, the ad will only generate more notoriety for Gehrig."[78]

Pollack insists that the ad can only benefit Gehrig's legend by raising more money at an especially critical time in ALS research. In the last decade, medical researchers have identified and isolated a gene that is involved in the inheritance of the disease, giving victims more hope than ever before that a cure can be found.[79] Under these circumstances, the former trial lawyer is optimistic that Gehrig will be vindicated. "Alcatel was the most lucrative licensing agreement we've ever done," he said, suggesting his ongoing partnership with the Gehrigs. "The fees that ad generates now or in the future will raise significant money for both ALS and muscular dystrophy at a time when the research is costing $20 million a year."

"I'm on safe ground saying that Lou and Eleanor Gehrig would want his image and name to be used for that purpose," insists Pollack, now in his late eighties. "Lou was a tremendously gifted man who received the dubious honor of having a disease named after him. What can be more fitting than to find a cure for the disease that claimed his life? I only hope that before I depart this life I can make that happen."[80]

## NOTES

1. Sean Kirst, "Hall of Immortals Didn't Live," *Syracuse Post Standard,* September 28, 1995.

2. National Baseball Hall of Fame Directors to Gerald F. Finley, Esq., Cooperstown, NY, August 16, 1941, National Baseball Hall of Fame Library.

3. Kirst, "Hall of Immortals Didn't Live."

4. Gallico, *Pride of the Yankees,* 162.

5. "Foster Field Names Athletic Park in Honor of Lou Gehrig," Press Release, May 29, 1942, National Baseball Hall of Fame Library.

6. Kevin Kernan, "Yanks Commemorate Legendary Lou Gehrig," *New York Post,* June 20, 2003.

7. "Biographical Data on Eleanor Gehrig," Muscular Dystrophy Association of America, Gehrig Estate.

8. Ibid.

9. Stanley W. Carlson, *Lou Gehrig: Baseball's Iron Man* (Minneapolis, MN: S.W. Carlson, 1941); Paul Gallico, *Lou Gehrig: Pride of the Yankees* (New York: Grosset and Dunlap, 1942); Frank Graham, *Lou Gehrig: A Quiet Hero* (New York: G.P. Putnam's Sons, 1942); and Richard Hubler, *Lou Gehrig: Iron Horse of Baseball* (Boston: Houghton Mifflin, 1941).

10. Gallico, *Pride of the Yankees,* 23–25.

11. Samuel Goldwyn quoted in Erickson, *Baseball in the Movies,* 247.

12. Ibid.

13. Creamer, *Babe,* 415–416.

14. Erickson, *Baseball in the Movies,* 247. Babe Dahlgren, who replaced Gehrig at first base when he retired, was also invited to play himself in the film, but Dahlgren was insulted by the $75 offer and declined. He later denounced Goldwyn as a "commercial leech" that was "capitalizing on a great man's name," because his replacement in the film was paid just about the same amount of money he was offered. (See Babe Dahlgren to Christy Walsh, February 25, 1942, National Baseball Hall of Fame Library.)

15. Kyle Crichton, "No Glamour Girl," *Collier's Weekly,* May 23, 1942, 13, 56; and Bill Francis, "Oscar Winner Attends Gehrig Event at Hall," *Freeman's Journal,* May 5, 2000. Wright believed that audiences wouldn't accept her in an older role because she had played children in her previous roles. Her film debut came in 1941, when she played Bette Davis' daughter in the screen adaptation of *The Little Foxes.*

16. Christy Walsh to Gentleman of the Press, October 2, 1941, New York, NY. National Baseball Hall of Fame; and Erickson, *Baseball in the Movies*, 246.

17. Erickson, *Baseball in the Movies*, 246; and Bak, *American Classic*, 175.

18. Erickson, *Baseball in the Movies*, 250; and Bak, *American Classic*, 176.

19. Kernan, "Yanks Commemorate Legendary Gehrig." The bracelet was made up of seventeen charms celebrating Gehrig's legendary career, including seven World championships and six All Star Games. Eleanor later presented it to the Hall of Fame where it remains a valued treasure.

20. Christy Walsh to Samuel Goldwyn, March 23, 1942, New York, NY; Christy Walsh to Eleanor Gehrig, March 23 and June 9, 1942, New York, NY; and Ben Washer to Eleanor Gehrig, April 2, 1942, Hollywood, CA. National Baseball Hall of Fame Library.

21. Interview with Teresa Wright, Yankee Stadium, Bronx, NY, June 19, 2003.

22. Erickson, *Baseball in the Movies*, 252; and Holtje, "Lou Gehrig" in Shatzkin, *Ballplayers*, 381. Holtje points out that the film shows Gehrig hitting a home run through the window of Columbia University's Low Library, which never happened. Also, Lou is portrayed as a lovable buffoon in many scenes, including those of a fraternity dance and his first appearance in a Yankee uniform.

23. Bak, *American Classic*, 179.

24. See "Pride of the Yankees" (1942), Reel Classics Web page, www.reelclassics.com/movies/yankees/yankees.htm 2002; Bob Kuenster, "These are Majors' Ten Best First Basemen of All Time," 64–66; and Jeff Idelson, "Teresa Wright, *Pride of the Yankees* Co-star, Offers Fond Memories of Legend," *Memories and Dreams*, 25, no. 2, Spring 2003, 18. In 1942 Teresa Wright was nominated for best actress for her role as Eleanor Gehrig in *Pride of the Yankees* and for best supporting actress for her role as Carol Beldon in the Academy Award–winning film *Mrs. Miniver*, also in 1942. Wright became just the second actress in history to be nominated for best actress and best supporting actress in the same year. Her last appearance came in *The Rainmaker* in 1997.

25. See records of Surrogate's Court, Bronx, NY, "Last Will and Testament of Henry Louis Gehrig," March 28, 1941, vol. 104, 485–489, Gehrig Estate.

26. See Supreme Court of New York, NY, "Henry and Christina Gehrig, Plaintiffs vs. Eleanor T. Gehrig," August 14, 1943, National Baseball Hall of Fame Library.

27. See Supreme Court of New York, NY, "Discontinuance of Henry and Christina Gehrig, Plaintiffs vs. Eleanor T. Gehrig," September 23, 1943, National Baseball Hall of Fame Library.

28. Milton M. Eisenburg [Gehrig Attorney], to Kensico Cemetery, July 23, 1944 and August 27, 1953, National Baseball Hall of Fame.

29. Kirst, "Hall of Immortals Didn't Live."

30. Muscular Dystrophy Association of America, "Biographical Data on Eleanor Gehrig."

31. "Lou Gehrig's Widow Pleads with Congress," *Washington Post*, May 11, 1949.

32. Ibid.

33. "A Scholarship Set Up for Columbia Students," *New York Times*, March 3, 1951.

34. Bak, *American Classic*, 168.

35. Robinson, *Iron Horse*, 282–283.

36. Pollack interview.

37. Bob Herzog, "Gehrig's Memory Alive," *Newsday*, September 7, 1995.

38. Pollack interview; and George Pollack to Arnie Mazur, November 19, 2000, Atlantic Beach, NY.

39. Pollack interview.

40. Shortly before he died, Lou contacted the book editor of the *New Yorker* to promote a writing career for his wife. (See Lou Gehrig to Clifton Fadiman, April 18, 1941, New York, NY, Gehrig files, National Baseball Hall of Fame and Library.)

41. When Pollack asked Eleanor why she wasn't more critical of Babe Ruth, she dismissed the question half-jokingly: "We all knew he drank all night and whored all night, but then he'd hit two home runs. How could I criticize the guy?" (See Weir, "Gehrig Wife Left Legacy.")

42. Gehrig and Durso, *My Luke and I*, 229.

43. Pollack interview.

44. Edward Herman quoted in Erickson, *Baseball in the Movies*, 203. Despite Herman's dissatisfaction with his portrayal of Gehrig, Eleanor complimented him on his low-key performance, saying it was much better than Gary Cooper's portrayal of a fun-loving Lou in *Pride of the Yankees.*

45. Ibid., 201–204; and Charles Witbeck, "NBC Gets Homer with Lou Gehrig's Story," *Utica [NY] Observer*, October 2, 1977.

46. Pollack interview.

47. Interview with Ray Robinson, New York, NY, June 12, 2003.

48. Joseph Durso, "Eleanor Gehrig, 79, Widow of Yankee Hall of Fame Star," *New York Times*, Obituary, March 8, 1984.

49. Pollack interview.

50. See Sonia Wedge to Paul Kerr, November 12, 1956, New York, NY, Gehrig files, National Baseball Hall of Fame Library.

51. "Estate of Christina Gehrig: Items left to the National Baseball Hall of Fame," November 1956, Gehrig files, National Baseball Hall of Fame Library.

52. Interview with Barry Halper, New York, NY, July 19, 2003. Halper discovered that Dahlgren had the glove while reading a *Sporting News* article. Dahlgren, according to the article, asked Gehrig for his glove on May 2, 1939, the day the Iron Horse took himself out of the line-up. Because Dahlgren was right-handed he never used the glove at first base, but he kept it as a memento of the great player he replaced. Halper contacted Dahlgren and asked to purchase the glove, which he did for $25,000, along with rare film footage of Dahlgren hitting the only Yankee home run in the 1939 World Series.

53. Pollack interview; Pollack to Arnie Mazur; and President George Bush, Sr. to Pollack, January 30, 1990, White House, Washington, DC.

54. Halper interview

55. Ray Robinson, *Iron Horse: Lou Gehrig in His Time* (New York: W.W. Norton, 1990).

56. Richard Bak, *Lou Gehrig: An American Classic* (Dallas, TX: Taylor Publishing, 1995).

57. Richard J. Tofel, *A Legend in the Making: The New York Yankees in 1939* (Chicago: Ivan R. Dee, 2002).

58. Norman L. Macht, *Baseball Legends: Lou Gehrig* (New York: Chelsea House, 1993); Richard Rambeck, *Lou Gehrig* (Mankato, MN: Child's World, 1994); and David A. Adler, *Lou Gehrig: The Luckiest Man* (San Diego: Harcourt Brace, 1997). These juvenile biographies are more sophisticated both in terms of narrative and illustrations than earlier books for youngsters, such as: Guernsey Van Riper, *Lou Gehrig: Boy of the Sandlots* (Indianapolis, IN: Bobbs-Merrill, 1949); Willard and Celia Luce, *Lou Gehrig: Iron Man of Baseball* (Champaign, IL: Garrard: 1970); Robert Rubin, *Lou Gehrig: Courageous Star* (New York: Putnam, 1979); and Keith Brandt, *Lou Gehrig: Pride of the Yankees* (Mahwah, NJ: Troll Associates, 1986).

59. See Pollack interview; George Pollack to Baseball Commissioner Allan H. Selig, August 22, 2002, Atlantic Beach, NY; and Bruce V. Bigelow, "ALS, Lou Gehrig and Baseball Cards," *Newsletter of the College of Physicians & Surgeons of Columbia University*, Spring 1997, 22. The Rip Van Winkle Foundation was founded in memory of Dr. Caldwell B. Esselstyn, the physician who treated Lou for ALS.

60. Pollack interview; and Herzog, "Gehrig's Memory Alive."

61. Pollack quoted in Bigelow, "ALS, Lou Gehrig and Baseball Cards"; Herzog, "Gehrig's Memory Alive"; and Weir, "Gehrig Wife Left Legacy."

62. Pollack interview.

63. Interview with Cal Ripken, Jr., Lutherville, MD, August 16, 2003.

64. Ibid.

65. Cal Ripken, Jr. quoted in ESPN Classics, *Sports Century: Lou Gehrig*.

66. Pollack quoted in Herzog, "Gehrig's Memory Alive."

67. See Lewis P. Rowland, MD, to George Pollack, March 14, 1996, New York, NY.

68. Mark Hyman, "$5,000 Seats Have a Grand View," *Baltimore Sun*, September 7, 1995.

69. Cal Ripken, Jr. quoted in "Cal Breaks Iron Horse's Record," *Baltimore Sun*, September 7, 1995.

70. Pollack interview.

71. Hyman, "$5,000 Seats Have a Grand View."

72. Phil Rogers, "Cal Ripken: More Than Baseball's Iron Man," *Baseball Digest*, September 2000, 56.

73. Williams, *Ted Williams' Hit List*, 56, 64. Williams ranked hitters on five factors: (1) intelligence at the plate, or making the pitcher work for his strikes; (2) courage, or the determination to hit the ball; (3) good eyesight, being able to identify a pitch once it leaves the pitcher's hand, especially the spin on a breaking ball; (4) power generated from the legs and hips as well as from the wrists and forearms; and (5) timing.

74. See Mark Vancil and Peter Hirdt, eds., *Major League Baseball's All-Century Team* (Chicago: Rare Air Media, 1999), 108–111.

75. See The Sporting News, *Baseball's 100 Greatest Players* (St. Louis, MO: The

Sporting News, 1998), 20–21; and "Fans Poll Results on the 50 Greatest Players of the Century," *Baseball Digest*, December 1999, 23–29. The *Sporting News* selection was made by the TSN staff and Gehrig finished sixth behind Ruth, Willie Mays, Ty Cobb, Walter Johnson, and Hank Aaron. The *Baseball Digest* selection was based on a poll of readers and Gehrig finished fifth behind Ruth, Mays, Cobb, and Ted Williams.

76. Michael McCarthy, "Alcatel to Use Gehrig's Famous Farewell in Ad," *USA Today*, April 17, 2001.

77. Ibid.

78. Brad Burns quoted in Richard Sandormir, "Gehrig's Digital Remake," *New York Times*, May 12, 2001.

79. In 1991 researchers discovered that the gene SOD1 is involved in inherited ALS. The gene is linked to chromosome 21, part of the cell structure that determines hereditary characteristics. A defect in this gene causes some cases of ALS. Additionally, evidence of similarities between ALS and two other incurable diseases—Alzheimer's and Parkinson's—gives hope that if a cure for one can be found, the others can also be treated. (See "New Understanding of ALS," *Mayo Clinic Health Letter*, April 1996, 5.)

80. Pollack interview.

# Epilogue: Honoring Lou's Legacy, 2003

When the novelist F. Scott Fitzgerald asked his readers to "show me a hero, and I'll show you a tragedy," he might well have anticipated Lou Gehrig's story.[1] Previous biographers have gone to great lengths to detail Gehrig's extraordinary ability on the playing field and his gentlemanly conduct off of it, as well as the tragedy of his untimely death. But there is a more elusive quality to Gehrig that still captures the public imagination more than sixty years after his death.

As a baseball historian, I've had the opportunity to meet and speak with many former major leaguers. Some admit to an understandable sense of loss when their careers are over. They experience all the emotions that come with that loss: denial, anger, and sadness. Some are able to come to terms with it. Others still live with one foot in the past, often because they just aren't able to find the same rush, the same kind of meaning in their post-baseball life. I'm sure Gehrig struggled with those feelings. But he was also able to move beyond them to make a meaningful contribution to humanity and one that still endures today in the fight against amyotrophic lateral sclerosis. The enduring nature of this contribution is the key to understanding Lou Gehrig's legend and legacy.

During the summer of 2003, the National ALS Association (ALSA) partnered with Major League Baseball, Minor League Baseball, and the National Baseball Hall of Fame to celebrate the 100th anniversary of Gehrig's birth. Researchers and physicians from North America, Britain, and France gathered at Tarrytown, New York, to commemorate the anniversary by holding a conference in which participants shared their ideas on how to improve and speed

Lou Gehrig watches the Yankees from the dugout in 1939. *National Baseball Hall of Fame Library, Cooperstown, N.Y.*

the implementation of clinical trials in ALS research.[2] Across the nation, major and minor league baseball teams conducted a variety of special events to benefit ALS research, including silent auctions, birthday parties, receptions, and private dinners. Profits from these events were donated to "The Lou Gehrig Challenge: The Campaign to Cure ALS," which raised a total of $25 million for research, patient and community services, public education, and advocacy.[3]

One of the most touching ceremonies occurred at Yankee Stadium on the morning of June 19. After the reading of a proclamation by the New York City Mayor's Office recognizing "Lou Gehrig Day" and some brief remarks by Tony Morante, New York Yankees' historian; Ray Robinson, Gehrig's biographer; and Dorine Gordon, president of the New York chapter of the ALS Association, members of the ALSA's Greater New York Chapter placed roses in front of Gehrig's monument. As he stood nearby, watching this simple but moving gesture, Robinson admitted how impressed he was by the large number of people "who seem to have an emotional connection to Gehrig, most of whom never saw him play." Robinson added, "When you stop to consider that he's been gone for over sixty years and that he was, after all, a baseball player and not a doctor, political leader or philosopher, it's pretty amazing to see how popular Gehrig remains."[4]

Dorine Gordon wasn't as surprised by the Iron Horse's enduring popularity. "Having Gehrig's name associated with ALS does help our cause," she said. It puts a face to the disease, helps to raise public awareness, and serves to inspire people with ALS and their families because Lou Gehrig's legacy is that of strength, courage, and a positive attitude in the face of adversity."[5]

Tony Morante, who leads tours for an average of 40,000 visitors each year through Monument Park, noted that the New York fans have a special reverence for the Iron Horse. "They tend to linger around his monument more than the others," he said, "probably because they know he was a New York City boy and was a standard bearer for the Yankees. Even the school children seem to know that he was special. You can see it in their eyes. That's why I try to make the connection between Lou and the importance he attached to education and hard work. Youngsters need to hear that. Hopefully, Gerhrig's example will inspire them, too."[6]

However, not all of the celebrants came from New York. Stuart Glassman, a New Hampshire physician and ALS advocate, attended the ceremony with his son Trevor, just as much to honor his own mother, Hilda, who died from ALS a few years earlier. "They both knew they were dying and yet neither of them ever asked for sympathy," he said, identifying the emotional bond that led him to his own commitment to find a cure for the disease. "Instead, they faced a certain death with dignity, and in this day and age you just don't see that very often."[7]

For those who celebrated the 100th anniversary of Gehrig's birth, what seemed to make his example so enduring was the sense that they could, in some way, relate to him. Gehrig was an ordinary person who was keenly aware of his human frailties and still managed to accomplish extraordinary things because he persevered. He displayed character in facing challenging obstacles throughout his life and career and perhaps for that reason alone, Gehrig remains a prototype for the American hero.

According to Joseph Campbell in his work *The Hero with a Thousand Faces*, the most enduring definition of a hero is one who "has been able to battle past their personal and historical limitations with grace and dignity to discover the true meaning of life," though there are no guarantees of a happy ending.[8] Such was the story of Gehrig's life.

Born in a tenement house on New York's Lower East Side, Gehrig grew up in poverty. He worked odd jobs to contribute to his German immigrant family's income, while struggling through school. Gehrig's hard work in the classroom and on the athletic field earned him a scholarship to Columbia University. Had his ailing parents not needed the money to pay medical bills, "Columbia Lou" might very well have completed his degree. Instead, he signed with the Yankees after his sophomore year in 1923, and made a virtue out of a necessity.

At 6 feet and 200 pounds, Gehrig was a strikingly handsome young man with a rock-solid physique that enabled him to become the premier clean-up hitter in the American League for most of his seventeen-year career. His statistical totals underscore his enduring status as an American sports hero. Year in and year out, he hit the ball with power, batted over .300, and almost always drove in more than 100 runs. He won five American League RBI titles and, in 1934, the coveted Triple Crown for leading the American League in batting average (.363), home runs (49), and RBIs (165). Just as impressive are his .340 lifetime average and 493 career home runs. With Gehrig as their clean-up hitter and first baseman, the Yankees captured seven pennants and six world championships.

From June 2, 1925, to May 2, 1939, when he benched himself "for the good of the team," Gehrig appeared in every game the Yankees played. Shaking off injuries, illnesses, and, in the last season of his career, even the crippling disease that ultimately claimed his life, Gehrig played in a total of 2,130 games. That record, which earned him the nickname "Iron Horse," stood for more than half a century. The streak also defined Gehrig's character as few records have defined any other professional athlete. His example of consistency, hard work, and sheer pride in performance endeared him to the common person.

Withdrawn, modest, and unassuming by nature, Gehrig was happy to surrender the spotlight to more flamboyant teammates like Babe Ruth and Joe DiMaggio. He accepted his subordinate position without envy or resentment, admitting that he wasn't "a headline guy, just the Yankee who's in there every day."[9]

At the same time, Ray Robinson reminds us that Gehrig "certainly was not a saint." Like other ballplayers, he "had his share of run-ins with umpires, participated in a few fights . . . was tight with his money . . . was moody, and occasionally indulged in unseemly practical jokes, much as the rambunctious Ruth did."[10] Despite these shortcomings, Gehrig was still the kind of role model that every parent wants for his child. Sadly, he was destined to a cruel fate.

That Gehrig should be cut down in the prime of his life by ALS is one of the most profound tragedies to befall an American sports hero. The disease, which has been described as being "present at your own funeral," sapped his remarkable strength, leaving him a shadow of the man he once was. Yet he confronted this nightmarish fate with grace and dignity. Instead of being bitter or trading on his name, he spent the last years of his life working for less than $6,000 a year as a New York City parole commissioner, writing letters of encouragement to other ALS victims, and cheering on his Yankees from the sidelines until his death on June 2, 1941. Afterwards, baseball and Hollywood used his example to generate the patriotism our country needed to overcome the hard times brought on by the Depression and World War II.

"If I could have been like any player in the history of baseball, it would be Lou Gehrig," admits Mike Schmidt, the Philadelphia Phillies' Hall of Fame third baseman and the 1983 recipient of the Lou Gehrig Award. "Not only did he play the game the way it's supposed to be played, but he was a *team* player, the epitome of class, dignity and just plain, old-fashioned hard work."[11] To be sure, Gehrig displayed a lot of class and dignity in the way he conducted his life, both on and off the field. But the Iron Horse's example continues to be so refreshing for an entire generation of people who never saw him play because they can relate to him.

Unlike so many other superstar athletes whom we've elevated as heroes, Gehrig never pretended to be anything more than a common person. He embodied an old-fashioned heroism that was grounded in the American ideal of sacrifice and the notion that hard work breeds success in life. Cal Ripken Jr., during his quest to break Gehrig's consecutive-game record, came to understand just how important that example was for fans. "In my travels across the nation during the streak, a lot of people related to me and to the streak in general because they saw 'showing up' as half the battle. While the fans still recognize and respect Lou's contributions on the field, I think they relate to his desire to be responsible every single day. Whether you're a ballplayer or a working person, there is a great deal of pride in going about your job each and every single day."[12]

What seems ironic is that Gehrig was born, raised, and lived his entire life in the spotlight of New York, a place that is not usually associated with mainstream American values. But baseball writer Jeff Silverman, a native New Yorker, disagrees, noting that part of Gehrig's appeal was that of the "hometown boy makes good." "For all of its flamboyance," he said, "New York is still just another American hometown full of ethnic groups, blue collars, and ordinary families. Gehrig grew up in an ethnic enclave, went to school in the city, stayed there for college, and signed with the hometown Yankees. He was 'one of us.' "[13]

Still, there is more to Gehrig's legend than old-fashioned heroism or the special affinity that the fans feel toward "one of their own." There was his courage and his humility. When Lou, in his farewell speech on July 4, 1939, called himself the "luckiest man on the face of the earth," he was appealing unwittingly to the humanity of the more than 61,000 people who packed Yankee Stadium that day as well as to thousands of others who were listening to the radio broadcast of the event. "All present in Yankee Stadium that day had been given a license to love a fellow human to the limit without qualification," wrote author Wilfrid Sheed, who was deeply moved by the speech. "If the Stadium had emptied out suddenly, and he had been left standing there alone, Gehrig would have felt no less lucky, because the appearance merely confirmed what he already knew, that he was having a good day . . . a day like that was worth a thousand of the old ones."[14]

Indeed, Gehrig reminded his listeners that all the fame and fortune he once enjoyed were not as important as the love of his family and friends. Those heartfelt sentiments, delivered by a dying hero, had such a profound effect on the crowd because as human beings we all agree that family and friends are the things that *really do matter most* in our own lives, yet we tend to place a lesser priority on them in our elusive quest for the kind of recognition and material affluence that Gehrig already possessed. That Lou Gehrig lived with courage and humility under difficult circumstances, and that he never lost sight of the truly important things in life is his legacy to us.

Perhaps, then, it is better to admire our heroes for their humanity than to revere them for their accomplishments. Only then can we do justice to their example and act on the better angels of our own nature.

## NOTES

1. F. Scott Fitzgerald, *The Crack-Up*, ed. Edmund Wilson (New York: J. Laughlin, 1945), iv.

2. See "Clinical Trials Are Focus of MDA ALS Conference," *The MDA/ALS Newsletter*, 8, no. 6, June 2003, 1; Columbia University College of Physicians & Surgeons and The Eleanor and Lou Gehrig MDA/ALS Research Center, "Lou Gehrig's Centennial Birthday: ALS Clinical Trials—The Challenge of the Next Century," Conference program at Dolce Tarrytown House, Tarrytown, NY, June 13–15, 2003.

3. Carole Coleman and Matt Burton, "Major League Baseball and the ALS Association Honor Lou Gehrig," News Release from Major League Baseball's Office of the Commissioner, New York, NY, June 16, 2003; and Jeff Snyder, "The ALS Association Joins with Major League Baseball to Raise Awareness of ALS in Commemoration of Baseball Legend Lou Gehrig's 100th Birthday Anniversary," News Release from the Amyotrophic Lateral Sclerosis Association, Calabasas Hills, CA, June 16, 2003.

4. Interview with Ray Robinson, Yankee Stadium, Bronx, NY, June 19, 2003.

5. Interview with Dorine Gordon, Yankee Stadium, Bronx, NY, June 19, 2003.

6. Interview with Tony Morante, Yankee Stadium, Bronx, NY, June 19, 2003.

7. Interview with Stuart Glassman, Yankee Stadium, Bronx, NY, June 19, 2003. In 1998 the Glassman family established the Hilda Glassman Award for Clinical Management Research. This award is given annually to one of the research projects approved for funding in the ALS Association's Clinical Management Research Grant Program.

8. Joseph Campbell, *The Hero with a Thousand Faces* (Princeton, NJ: Princeton University Press, 1968).

9. Donald Honig, *The Power Hitters* (St. Louis, MO: The Sporting News, 1989), 35.

10. Ray Robinson, "Birthday Party For 'Luckiest Man,' Game's Durable Icon," *New York Times*, June 15, 2003.

11. Interview with Mike Schmidt, Jupiter, FL, June 10, 2003.

12. Cal Ripkin, Jr., interview.

13. Interview with Jeff Silverman, West Chester, PA, June 13, 2003.

14. Wilfrid Sheed quoted in Ray Robinson, "Remembering Lou Gehrig," *Memories and Dreams*, 25, no. 2, Spring 2003, 14–15.

# APPENDIX: LOU GEHRIG'S CAREER AND WORLD SERIES STATISTICS

## Career Statistics

| Year | Club | League | G | AB | R | H | 2B | 3B | HR | RBI | BA | PO | A | E | FA |
|---|---|---|---|---|---|---|---|---|---|---|---|---|---|---|---|
| 1921 | Hartford | Eastern | 12 | 46 | 5 | 12 | 1 | 2 | 0 | — | .261 | 130 | 4 | 2 | .985 |
| 1922 | Not in Organized Ball | | | | | | | | | | | | | | |
| 1923 | New York | American | 13 | 26 | 6 | 11 | 4 | 1 | 1 | 9 | .423 | 53 | 3 | 4 | .933 |
| 1923 | Hartford | Eastern | 59 | 227 | 54 | 69 | 13 | 8 | 24 | — | .304 | 623 | 23 | 6 | .991 |
| 1924 | New York | American | 10 | 12 | 2 | 6 | 1 | 0 | 0 | 5 | .500 | 10 | 1 | 0 | 1.000 |
| 1924 | Hartford | Eastern | 134 | 504 | 111 | 186 | 40 | 13 | 37 | — | .369 | 1391 | 66 | 23** | .984 |
| 1925 | New York | American | 126 | 437 | 73 | 129 | 23 | 10 | 20 | 68 | .295 | 1126 | 53 | 13 | .989 |
| 1926 | New York | American | 155 | 572 | 135 | 179 | 47 | 20* | 16 | 107 | .313 | 1566 | 73 | 15 | .991 |
| 1927 | New York | American | 155* | 584 | 149 | 218 | 52* | 18 | 47 | 175* | .373 | 1662* | 88 | 15 | .992 |
| 1928 | New York | American | 154 | 562 | 139 | 210 | 47** | 13 | 27 | 142** | .374 | 1488* | 79 | 18* | .989 |
| 1929 | New York | American | 154 | 553 | 127 | 166 | 32 | 10 | 35 | 126 | .300 | 1458 | 82 | 9 | .994 |
| 1930 | New York | American | 154** | 581 | 143 | 220 | 42 | 17 | 41 | 174* | .379 | 1298 | 89* | 15 | .989 |
| 1931 | New York | American | 155 | 619 | 163* | 211* | 31 | 15 | 46** | 184* | .341 | 1352 | 58 | 13 | .991 |
| 1932 | New York | American | 156* | 596 | 138 | 208 | 42 | 9 | 34 | 151 | .349 | 1293 | 75 | 18 | .987 |
| 1933 | New York | American | 152 | 593 | 138* | 198 | 41 | 12 | 32 | 139 | .334 | 1290 | 64 | 9 | .993 |
| 1934 | New York | American | 154* | 579 | 128 | 210 | 40 | 6 | 49* | 165* | .363* | 1284 | 80 | 8 | .994 |
| 1935 | New York | American | 149 | 535 | 125* | 176 | 26 | 10 | 30 | 119 | .329 | 1337 | 82 | 15 | .990 |
| 1936 | New York | American | 155** | 579 | 167* | 205 | 37 | 7 | 49* | 152 | .354 | 1377 | 82 | 9 | .994 |
| 1937 | New York | American | 157* | 569 | 138 | 200 | 37 | 9 | 37 | 159 | .351 | 1370 | 74 | 16* | .989 |
| 1938 | New York | American | 157** | 576 | 115 | 170 | 32 | 6 | 29 | 114 | .295 | 1483 | 100 | 14 | .991 |
| 1939 | New York | American | 8 | 28 | 2 | 4 | 0 | 0 | 0 | 1 | .143 | 64 | 4 | 2 | .971 |
| Major League Totals— | | 17 years | 2164 | 8001 | 1888 | 2721 | 534 | 163 | 493 | 1990 | .340 | 19511 | 1087 | 193 | .991 |
| Minor League Totals— | | 3 years | 205 | 777 | 170 | 267 | 54 | 23 | 61 | — | .311 | 2144 | 93 | 91 | .987 |

* indicates league leader
** indicates tied for league lead
A = assists; AB = at-bats; BA = batting average; E = errors; FA = fielding average; G = games; H = hits; HR = home runs; PO = put-outs; R = runs; RBI = runs batted in; 2B = doubles; 3B = triples

World Series Statistics

| Year | Club | G | AB | R | H | 2B | 3B | HR | RBI | BA | PO | A | E | FA |
|---|---|---|---|---|---|---|---|---|---|---|---|---|---|---|
| 1926 | New York | 7 | 23 | 1 | 8 | 2 | 0 | 0 | 3 | .348 | 78 | 1 | 0 | 1.000 |
| 1927 | New York | 4 | 13 | 2 | 4 | 2 | 2 | 0 | 4 | .308 | 41 | 3 | 0 | 1.000 |
| 1928 | New York | 4 | 11 | 5 | 6 | 1 | 0 | 4 | 9 | .545 | 33 | 0 | 0 | 1.000 |
| 1932 | New York | 4 | 17 | 9 | 9 | 1 | 0 | 3 | 8 | .529 | 37 | 2 | 1 | .975 |
| 1936 | New York | 6 | 24 | 5 | 7 | 1 | 0 | 2 | 7 | .292 | 45 | 2 | 0 | 1.000 |
| 1937 | New York | 5 | 17 | 4 | 5 | 1 | 1 | 1 | 3 | .294 | 50 | 1 | 0 | 1.000 |
| 1938 | New York | 4 | 14 | 4 | 4 | 0 | 0 | 0 | 0 | .286 | 25 | 3 | 0 | 1.000 |
| Totals—7 years | | 34 | 119 | 30 | 43 | 8 | 3 | 10 | 34 | .361 | 309 | 12 | 1 | .997 |

*Source*: Rick Wolff, ed., *The Baseball Encyclopedia* (New York: Macmillan Publishing Co. 1990, 8th edition), 936.

# A Note about Lou Gehrig's Disease

Today, the need to find a cure for amyotrophic lateral sclerosis (ALS) is more pressing than ever before. As many as 30,000 Americans are currently affected by the neurodegenerative disease and an average of fifteen people are diagnosed with ALS each day, more than 5,600 a year. Since 1991, the national ALS Association (ALSA), the largest private source of funding for ALS-specific research in the world, has raised more than $50 million to fund research, treat the debilitating effects of the disease, and improve the quality of life for those who struggle with it. But the cost to patients' families is enormous, averaging up to $200,000 per year. To find out more about an ALSA chapter in your area, call (818) 880-9007, or visit the ALSA Web site at www.alsa.org.

# Bibliography

## Biographies of Lou Gehrig

Bak, Richard. *Lou Gehrig: An American Classic*. Dallas: Taylor, 1995.

Carlson, Stanley W. *Lou Gehrig: Baseball's Iron Man*. Minneapolis: S.W. Carlson, 1941.

Gallico, Paul. *Lou Gehrig: Pride of the Yankees*. New York: Grosset & Dunlap, 1942.

Gehrig, Eleanor, and Joseph Durso. *My Luke and I*. New York: Thomas Y. Crowell, 1976.

Graham, Frank. *Lou Gehrig: A Quiet Hero*. New York: G.P. Putnam's Sons, 1942.

Hubler, Richard. *Lou Gehrig: The Iron Horse of Baseball*. Boston: Houghton Mifflin, 1941.

Robinson, Ray. *Iron Horse: Lou Gehrig and His Time*. New York: Oxford University Press, 1990.

## Juvenile Biographies of Lou Gehrig

Adler, David A. *Lou Gehrig: The Luckiest Man*. San Diego: Harcourt Brace, 1997.

Brandt, Keith, and John Lawn. *Lou Gehrig: Pride of the Yankees*. New York: Demco Media, 1986.

Luce, Willard, and Celia Luce. *Lou Gehrig: Iron Man of Baseball*. New York: Garrard Publishing Company, 1970.

Macht, Norman L. *Baseball Legends: Lou Gehrig*. New York: Chelsea House, 1993.

Rambeck, Richard. *Lou Gehrig*. New York: Child's World, 1994.

Rubin, Robert. *Lou Gehrig: Courageous Star*. New York: Putnam, 1979.

Van Riper, Guernsey. *Lou Gehrig: Boy of the Sandlots*. New York: Bobbs-Merrill, 1949.

# Bibliography

## BOOKS

Alexander, Charles C. *John McGraw*. New York: Penguin, 1989.

Allen, Maury. *Where Have You Gone, Joe DiMaggio? The Story of America's Last Hero*. New York: Dutton, 1975.

Anderson, Dave, et al. *The New York Yankees: An Illustrated History*. New York: St. Martin's Press, 2002.

Berrol, Selma. *The Empire City: New York and Its People, 1624–1996*. Westport, CT: Praeger, 1997.

Bevis, Charlie. *Mickey Cochrane: The Life of a Baseball Hall of Fame Catcher*. Jefferson, NC: McFarland, 1998.

Cox, James A. *The Lively Ball: Baseball in the Roaring Twenties*. Alexandria, VA: Redefinition Books, 1989.

Cramer, Richard Ben. *Joe DiMaggio: The Hero's Life*. New York: Simon & Schuster, 2000.

Creamer, Robert W. *Babe: The Legend Comes to Life*. New York: Simon & Schuster, 1974.

Erickson, Hal. *Baseball in the Movies: A Comprehensive Reference, 1915–1991*. Jefferson, NC: McFarland, 1992.

Fass, Paula S. *The Damned and the Beautiful: American Youth in the 1920s*. New York: Oxford University Press, 1977.

Fleming, G. H. *Murderer's Row: The 1927 New York Yankees*. New York: William Morrow, 1985.

Gallagher, Mark, and Walter LaConte. *The Yankee Encyclopedia*. 5th ed. New York: Sports Publishing, 2001.

Greenberg, Hank, with Ira Berkow. *Hank Greenberg: The Story of My Life*. New York: Times Books, 1989.

Handlin, Oscar. *The Uprooted*. 2nd ed. Boston: Little, Brown & Co., 1973.

Henrich, Tommy, and Bill Glibert. *Five O'Clock Lightening: Ruth, Gehrig, DiMaggio, Mantle and the Glory Years of the New York Yankees*. New York: Crown, 1992.

Hollingsworth, Harry. *The Best & Worst Baseball Teams of All Time*. New York: SPI Books, 1994.

Honig, Donald. *Baseball's 10 Greatest Teams*. New York: Macmillan, 1982.

———. *The Power Hitters*. St. Louis: The Sporting News, 1989.

Jackson, Kenneth T., and David S. Dunbar. *Empire City: New York through the Centuries*. New York: Columbia University Press, 2002.

Kashatus, William C. *Connie Mack's '29 Triumph: The Rise and Fall of the Philadelphia Athletics Dynasty*. Jefferson, NC: McFarland, 1999.

Kohout, Martin Donell. *Hal Chase: The Defiant Life and Turbulent Times of Baseball's Biggest Crook*. Jefferson, NC: McFarland, 2001.

Luebke, Frederick C. *Bonds of Loyalty: German-Americans and World War I*. DeKalb: Northern Illinois University Press, 1974.

Neft, David S., et al. *The Sports Encyclopedia: Baseball.* New York: Grosset & Dunlap, 1974.

Neyer, Rob, and Eddie Epstein. *Baseball Dynasties: The Greatest Teams of All Time.* New York: W.W. Norton, 2000.

Reidenbaugh, Lowell. *The Sporting News Selects Baseball's 25 Greatest Teams.* St. Louis: The Sporting News, 1988.

Ritter, Lawrence. *The Glory of Their Times: The Story of the Early Days of Baseball Told by the Men Who Played It.* New York: Vintage, 1985.

———. *Lost Ballparks: A Celebration of Baseball's Legendary Fields.* New York: Viking Studio Books, 1992.

Ruth, Babe. *The Babe Ruth Story.* New York: Dutton, 1948; reprinted by Penguin 1992.

Schoener, Allon. *New York: An Illustrated History of the People.* New York: W.W. Norton, 1998.

Schoor, Gene. *The History of the World Series.* New York: William Morrow, 1990.

Smelser, Marshall. *The Life That Ruth Built: A Biography.* New York: Quadrangle, 1975.

Smith, Ron. *The Sporting News Selects Baseball's 100 Greatest Players.* St. Louis: The Sporting News, 1998.

Stout, Glenn, and Richard A. Johnson. *Yankees Century: 100 Years of New York Yankees Baseball.* Boston: Houghton Mifflin, 2002.

Tofel, Richard J. *A Legend in the Making: The New York Yankees in 1939.* Chicago: Ivan R. Dee, 2002.

Trachtenberg, Leo. *The Wonder Team: The True Story of the Incomparable 1927 New York Yankees.* Bowling Green, OH: Bowling Green State University, 1995.

Vancil, Mark, and Peter Hirdt, eds. *Major League Baseball's All-Century Team.* Chicago: Rare Air Media, 1999.

White, G. Edward. *Creating the National Pastime: Baseball Transforms Itself, 1903–1953.* Princeton, NJ: Princeton University Press, 1996.

Williams, Ted, and Jim Prime. *Ted Williams' Hit List.* Indianapolis, IN: Masters Press, 1996.

## ARTICLES AND CHAPTERS

Arbolino, Jack N. "The Lion Afield." In *A History of Columbia College on Morningside.* New York: Columbia University Press, 1954.

Bigelow, Bruce V. "ALS Lou Gehrig and Baseball Cards." *Newsletter of the College of Physicians & Surgeons of Columbia University* (Spring 1997).

Boardman, Fon W., Jr. "After Class." In *A History of Columbia College on Morningside.* New York: Columbia University Press, 1954.

Brundidge, Harry T. "Gehrig Gives Baseball Full Credit for Rescuing Parents and Self from New York Tenement District." *Sporting News* (December 25, 1930).

"Cal Breaks Iron Horse's Record." *Baltimore Sun* (September 7, 1995).

Chellgren, Norton. "Gehrig's Debut Was Strictly on the Sly." *Washington Times* (April 23, 1986).

Considine, Bob. "John Kieran: Sage of Rockport." *Boston Herald American* (April 18, 1975).

Crichton, Kyle. "No Glamour Girl." *Collier's Weekly* (May 23, 1942).

Daniel, Dan. "Doctors Say Tiny Ticker Gives Lou Durability." *New York World Telegram* (September 30, 1936).

———. " 'Not Through!' Says Gehrig." *New York World Telegram* (April 28, 1939).

Dolgan, Bob. "Iron Man Lou Gehrig Played in the Shadow of Babe Ruth." *Baseball Digest* (November 1995).

Durso, Joseph. "Eleanor Gehrig, 79, Widow of Yankee Hall of Fame Star." *New York Times* (Obituary) (March 8, 1984).

Francis, Bill. "Oscar Winner Attends Gehrig Event at Hall." *Freeman's Journal* (May 5, 2000).

Frank, Stanley. "Gehrig Ran Out on First Game." *New York Post* (August 7, 1934).

———. "Tribute Paid to the Iron Horse Has No Equal in Baseball." *New York Times* (July 5, 1939).

Fullerton, Hugh. "Gehrig Biggest Star in College Baseball." *New York Tribune* (April 29, 1923).

Gallagher, Tom, and Christopher D. Renino. "Babe Ruth." In *The Ballplayers: Baseball's Ultimate Biographical Reference*, edited by Mike Shatzkin. New York: William Morrow, 1990.

"Gehrig, Iron Man of Baseball Dies at the Age of 37." *New York Times* (June 3, 1941).

Gehrig, Lou. "Am I Jealous of Babe Ruth?" In Gehrig Files, National Baseball Hall of Fame Library, 1933.

"Gehrig Eclipses Scott's Record Playing 1,308th Straight Game." *New York Times* (August 18, 1933).

"Gehrig Hitting Maniac Since 'Beaning.' " *New York World Telegram* (August 6, 1934).

"Gehrig Ready for 'Check-up.' " *New York Times* (June 13, 1939).

"Gehrig Strikes Out Seventeen Batters, But Columbia Nine Loses to Williams, 5–1." *New York Tribune* (April 19, 1923).

"Gehrig Thinks He Is Winning." *New York World Telegram* (January 30, 1941).

"Gehrig Wins Triple Honors." *The Sporting News* (December 6, 1934).

Gerlach, Larry R. "German Americans in Major League Baseball: Sport and Acculturation." In *The American Game: Baseball and Ethnicity*, edited by Lawrence Baldassaro and Richard A. Johnson. Carbondale: Southern Illinois University Press, 2002.

Hallman, Don. "DiMaggio Hits 3, Yanks Win, 14–5." *New York Daily News* (May 4, 1936).

" 'Hardest Hitter Ever,' Says Coakley of Young Gehrig." *New York World Telegram* (June 17, 1923).

Harwell, Ernie. "Wally Pipp's Big League Career Forgotten with a 'Headache.' " *Baseball Digest* (September 2000).

Herzog, Bob. "Gehrig's Memory Alive." *Newsday* (September 7, 1995).

Holtje, Stephen. "Lou Gehrig." In *The Ballplayers: Baseball's Ultimate Biographical Reference,* edited by Mike Shatzkin. New York: William Morrow, 1990.

Idelson, Jeff. "Teresa Wright, *Pride of the Yankees* Co-Star, Offers Fond Memories of Legend." *Memories and Dreams,* 25, no. 2 (Spring 2003).

Kasarskis, Edward, and Mary Winslow. "When Did Lou Gehrig's Personal Illness Begin?" *Neurology* (1989).

Kavanagh, Jack. "Andy Coakley." In *The Ballplayers: Baseball's Ultimate Biographical Reference,* edited by Mike Shatzkin. New York: William Morrow, 1990.

Kernan, Kevin. "Yanks Commemorate Legendary Lou Gehrig." *New York Post* (June 20, 2003).

Kieran, John. "Huggins Sends in Youngsters to Beat Washington." *New York Herald Tribune* (June 3, 1925).

Kirst, Sean. "Hall of Immortals Didn't Live." *Syracuse (NY) Post Standard* (September 28, 1995).

Kuenster, Bob. "These Are Majors' Ten Best First Basemen of All Time." *Baseball Digest* (July 1994).

Lieb, Frederick G. "Baseball—The Nation's Melting Pot." *Baseball Magazine* (August 1923).

"Lou Gehrig Has Paralysis, Career with Yanks Ends." *Cleveland News* (June 22, 1939).

"Lou Gehrig Named to the Hall of Fame." *New York Daily News* (December 8, 1939).

"Lou Gehrig's Widow Pleads with Congress." *Washington Post* (May 11, 1949).

Martin, Whitney. "Doctors Say Lou Must Retire to Conserve Energy." *Philadelphia Inquirer* (June 22, 1939).

McCann, Dick. "Gehrig Funeral This Morning." *New York Daily News* (June 4, 1941).

McCarthy, Michael. "Alcatel to Use Gehrig's Famous Farewell in Ad." *USA Today* (April 17, 2001).

Miley, Jack. "Fun-Loving Guy Brings a Smile to Lou's Face." *New York Daily News* (July 5, 1939).

Murphy, Edward T. "Gehrig Proves Real Iron Man as He Fights to Overcome Ailment." *New York Sun* (June 22, 1939).

"No Other Player to Use Gehrig's Number or Locker." *New York Times* (January 6, 1940).

"Physicians Baffled by 'Gehrig's Disease.' " *New York World Telegram* (June 4, 1941).

Povich, Shirley. " 'Iron Horse' Breaks As Athletic Greats Meet in His Honor." *Washington Post* (July 5, 1939).

Powers, Jimmy. "Babe Picks Successor." *New York Daily News* (August 29, 1937).

———. "Has 'Polio' Hit the Yankees?" *New York Daily News* (August 18, 1940).

———. "Our Apologies to Lou Gehrig and the Yankees." *New York Daily News* (September 26, 1940).

———. "Paralysis Ends Gehrig's Career." *New York Daily News* (June 22, 1939).

Richman, Milton. "Mrs. Gehrig Likes to Talk About Lou." *New York Daily News* (August 8, 1973).

Robinson, Ray. "Birthday Party For 'Luckiest Man,' Game's Durable Icon." *New York Times* (June 15, 2003).

———. "Lou Gehrig: Columbia Legend and American Hero." *Columbia University Alumni Magazine* (Fall 2001).

———. "Remembering Lou Gehrig." *Memories and Dreams*, 25, no. 2 (Spring 2003).

———. "Ruth & Gehrig: Friction Between Gods." *New York Times* (June 2, 1991).

Rogers, Phil. "Cal Ripken: More than Baseball's Iron Man." *Baseball Digest* (September 2000).

Sandormir, Richard. "Gehrig's Digital Remake." *New York Times* (May 12, 2001).

"A Scholarship Set Up for Columbia Students." *New York Times* (March 3, 1951).

Schultz, Randy. "Gehrig Wasn't Defined by Streak." *Sporting News* (June 19, 1989).

Slocum, Bill. "Gehrig Leads HR Race." *New York American* (May 8, 1927).

Suehsdorf, A. D. "Miller Huggins." In *The Ballplayers: Baseball's Ultimate Biographical Reference*, edited by Mike Shatzkin. New York: William Morrow, 1990.

Topel, Brett. "Yankee Teammates Recall the Greatness of Lou Gehrig." *Baseball Digest* (July 1995).

Watson, Tom. "Dying Yankee Legend Came Here to Help Kids." *Riverdale Press* (June 8, 1989).

Weir, Tom. "Gehrig's Wife Left Legacy of Uncommon Memories." *USA Today* (September 1, 1995).

Williams, Joe. "McCarthy Admits Doubt About Gehrig in '39 Yank Set Up." *New York World Telegram* (March 16, 1939).

Witbeck, Charles. "NBC Gets Homer with Lou Gehrig's Story." *Utica (NY) Observer* (October 2, 1977).

## FILMS, VIDEOS, AND WEB SITES

Limmer, Ruth, and Andrew S. Dolkart. "The Tenement As History and Housing." Tenement Museum of New York Web site: http://www.tenement.org.

"Lou Gehrig." The Baseball Page Web site: http://www.thebaseballpage.com.

*Pride of the Yankees* (1942) Reel Classics Web page: http://www.reelclassics.com.

"Sports Century: Lou Gehrig." ESPN Classics Video, 2000.

# Index

## About the Author

WILLIAM C. KASHATUS is a professional historian and educator who holds a doctorate from the University of Pennsylvania. Kashatus has written for the *New York Times*, *Philadelphia Daily News*, and *St. Louis Post-Dispatch*, among other publications. His previous baseball books include *September Swoon: Richie Allen, the '64 Phillies, and Racial Integration*; *Mike Schmidt: Philadelphia's Hall of Fame Third Baseman*; *Connie Mack's '29 Triumph: The Rise and Fall of the Philadelphia Athletics Dynasty*; and *One-Armed Wonder: Pete Gray, Wartime Baseball, and the American Dream*. He lives in Chester County, Pennsylvania.